365

Motifs for
Every Mood &
Every Occasion

CROSS-STITCH

Jennifer Dargel

C&T PUBLISHING
Another Maker Inspired!

FRECH*
WILD
WUNDER
BAR *

ANNA
&
BEN

365

Motifs for Every Mood & Every Occasion

CROSS-STITCH

Jennifer Dargel

ALL THE BASICS *and a variety of sizes*

CONTENTS

Introduction   6

The Basics   *8*

Materials & Equipment   10

Before Starting ...   16

Helpful Tips   18

Cross-Stitch Technique   19

Finishing Off   20

Patterns   *22*

Flowers & Wreaths   24

Letters & Sayings   38

Nature & Plants   66

Children's Bedroom   80

Food & Kitchen   92

Geometric Animals   100

Abstract Art   104

Colors & Shapes   118

Traditional Designs   132

Seasons & Holidays   140

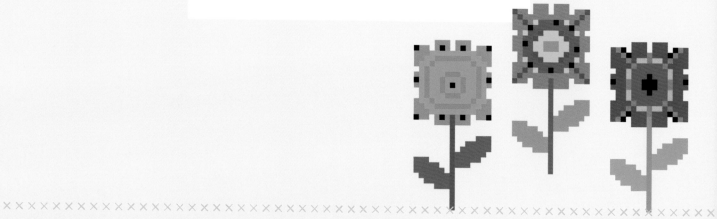

My Own Designs   **158**

....   160

....   161

....   162

....   163

....   164

....   165

....   166

....   167

Color Table   **168**

About the Author   **172**

Acknowledgements   **173**

INTRODUCTION

This book is for anyone who wants to get creative with stitching. Beginners will find valuable tips and instructions on all things embroidery, while those who are more advanced will find a colorful collection of creative and modern ideas that can all be completed with a single embroidery technique—the cross-stitch.

I designed this book to encourage you to use your imagination. The patterns can be mixed together to create unique individual pieces by using the embroidery alphabet to make various sayings and names. In addition, motifs have been designed in the same or similar color families so they can be easily combined. You can always start with one design and then go a step further by adding another motif from this series. For me, it was also important that you could embroider several motifs even with a small color palette—great for beginners!

The different themes range from flowers to sayings to geometric animals. There's really something for every taste and occasion, whether you intend to keep your finished piece or give it to someone else.

My goal was to create a DIY book full of modern cross-stitch art, joy, inspiration, and super easy instructions to prove that this traditional craft is definitely not outdated. This book gives a simple and inspiring introduction to a hobby that requires only four items: a needle, thread, embroidery hoop, and fabric. It's time to get creative!

Have fun with your cross-stitch and enjoy a little relaxation!

from Sonntagskreativität (Sunday Creativity)

THE BASICS

MATERIALS & EQUIPMENT

Embroidery Floss

Embroidery floss is available in different varieties and colors.

Embroidery Floss (1)

Embroidery floss is made up of 6 intertwined threads and is probably the most commonly used of all embroidery floss. The shiny threads are excellent for embroidery projects. Embroidery floss comes in skeins of 8m (8¾yds) each with an extensive color palette. I worked exclusively with Stranded Cotton by Anchor in this book. (Pictured: Stranded Cotton by Anchor)

Perle Cotton

This is even shinier than embroidery floss and is made up of 2 strands of cotton. Perle cotton is also suitable for cross-stitch projects but is thicker, as this thread cannot be split.

Metallic Cotton (2)

Metallic cotton is suitable for adding accents and giving your designs a glittery effect. However, it is usually a bit more difficult to work with, so it's best to only use it selectively.

Matte Embroidery Thread (3)

This thread has a wool-like structure and is thicker than embroidery floss despite having only 5 strands. It has a matte finish and is 100% cotton. This is better suited for larger-count fabrics. (Pictured: Soft Embroidery thread by Anchor)

Embroidery Hoops

Embroidery hoops come in many sizes and are available in beechwood, bamboo, and plastic. The most common ones have a diameter between 4–10 in (10–25cm), but there are also smaller and larger hoops. In this book, I worked with hoops measuring 5″ (13cm), 7″ (16cm), and 8″ (19cm).

Beechwood Embroidery Hoops (4)

Natural-colored beechwood is finely sanded and tripled glued, and offers a high-quality standard. The fabric is stretched in the frame and is fixed in place with the brass adjusting screw to maintain the tension required to start embroidering.

Bamboo Embroidery Hoops

A bamboo hoop is a slightly less expensive option but is still suitable for all kinds of embroidery projects. Bamboo hoops are lighter in color and usually have a stainless steel adjusting screw.

Plastic Embroidery Hoops

These are available in a range of colors and can therefore add a color accent.

Thread Box (5)

You can store all your embroidery floss neatly and arrange it by color or number in a practical thread box. Simply wind the thread around the "thread cards," which are available in paper or plastic.

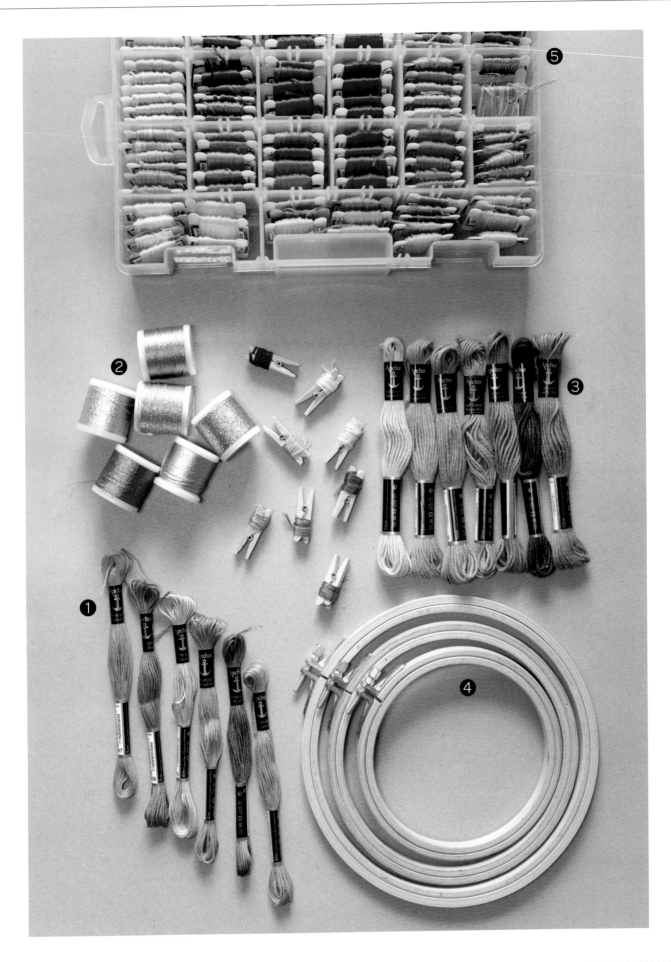

Fabrics

There are lots of different embroidery fabrics that vary depending on the project. I only suggest "counted" fabrics here, as these are needed for cross-stitch.

Aida Cloth

Made of cotton or linen, this is probably the most well-known counted fabric. It's very popular with beginners, as it's really easy to see and count the individual squares. The size of the fabric is given in stitches per inch; one fabric may have 16 stitches per inch, while another may only have 6 stitches per inch. Even though you can embroider the designs from this book on a wide variety of counted fabrics, it's important to consider the size of the project. Beginners should keep in mind that the smaller the number of stitches per inch, the easier (but also larger) the project will be.

Linen

Linen is finer than Aida fabrics, but the squares are not so clearly visible. It's good to use for cross-stitch but isn't recommended for beginners because of its structure.

Canvas

Canvas is woven with only 2 threads and is easy to embroider with wool or matte embroidery threads. It is suitable for children's projects thanks to its very coarse structure.

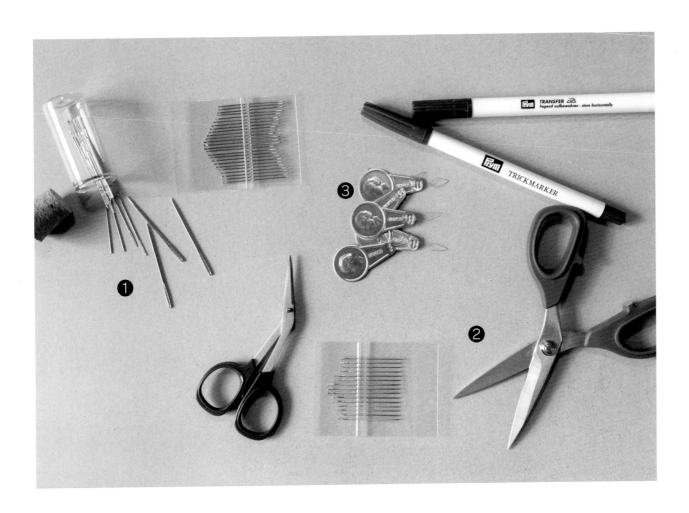

Other Embroidery Accessories

Tapestry Needle (1)

For cross-stitch projects, you need a tapestry needle without a point. The size of the needle depends on the size of the fabric and how many threads you want to use. If you want to try out different options, you can buy needle sets that contain several needle sizes.

Scissors (2)

Small, pointed scissors and large fabric scissors are required.

Threading Aid (3)

This tool makes it easier to thread up the needle, especially for beginners. The floss is pulled through the wire loop and can then be threaded more easily into the smaller eye of the needle.

Marker Pens

Even though it is unusual, I tend to draw the counting motif onto the fabric before I start. It makes the embroidery easier since you no longer have to count, but it is a personal choice and isn't always necessary. There are different markers that disappear when exposed to heat, light, or water. Cross-stitch traditionally involves counting while embroidering without pre-marking, but just see which way you find easier.

Other Tools

Cardstock

... I cut the card into shape with the help of the embroidery hoop and glue it to the back of my project if the finished piece is being displayed on the wall in the hoop.

Craft or Fabric Glue

... I use this to glue the back side of the fabric.

Screwdriver

... I use this once the fabric is placed in the embroidery hoop if I need to readjust the tension in the hoop.

BEFORE STARTING...

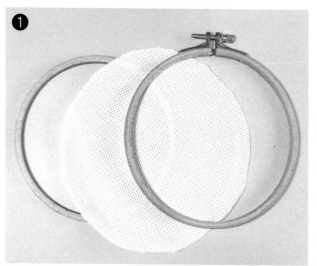

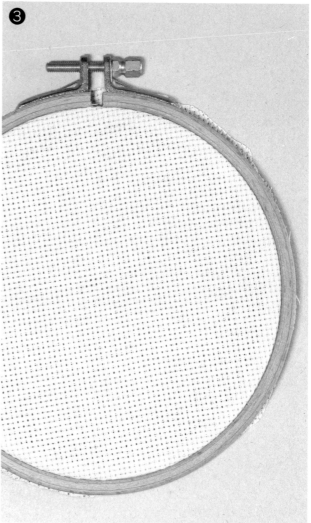

Securing the fabric in the embroidery hoop

1. Place the inside ring on the table, lay the fabric over it, place the outside ring with the adjusting screw on top of it, and press into place.

2. Tighten the adjusting screw.

3. Gently pull the edges of the fabric all around to tighten it, and readjust the screw if necessary.

Divide the embroidery floss

Classic embroidery floss consists of 6 individual strands that can be divided as desired for different projects and fabrics. To do this, gently pull the thread apart. It's important to divide the thread carefully; otherwise, it will get knotted.

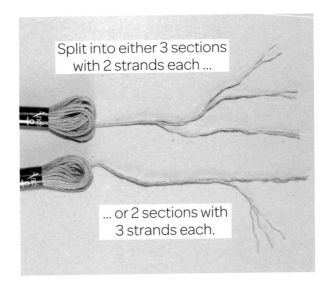

Split into either 3 sections with 2 strands each ...

... or 2 sections with 3 strands each.

Knotting the thread

There are two different ways to knot the thread.

1. The first way is to tie a simple knot at the end of the thread. Make sure that there isn't too much thread left behind the knot; otherwise, it will quickly pull forward again when you do the next stitches.

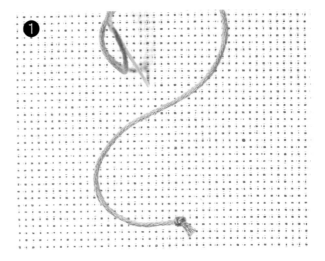

2. The second way is to not pull the thread all the way through on the first stitch and leave a little bit on the back. Then you can stitch over this with your next stitches to fix it in place.

HELPFUL TIPS

1 If you've never picked up an embroidery needle before, you should start off with a small, manageable project with an appropriate level of difficulty. All of the projects here are suitable for beginners, but embroidery can take a while, so it's nice to see "quick" successes, particularly at the beginning.

2 Cut the thread into lengths of around 12″ (30cm) to prevent it from knotting faster.

3 You can skip (leave blank) up to three squares. For a longer distance, I would recommend knotting the thread and starting over.

4 Make sure that your fabric always remains taut in the embroidery hoop. Rather than working with fabric that is too loose, it's better to readjust the fabric and tighten the adjusting screw. The tighter your fabric is secured, the easier it will be to embroider.

5 Take your time. Embroidery is not a quick task, but you'll soon get into the flow if you put your mind to it.

6 Cut the fabric all around, leaving at least a 1″ (2.2cm) overhang so that you have enough fabric to reposition your design in the embroidery hoop if necessary. You can cut off the rest, as it will only interfere with the embroidery.

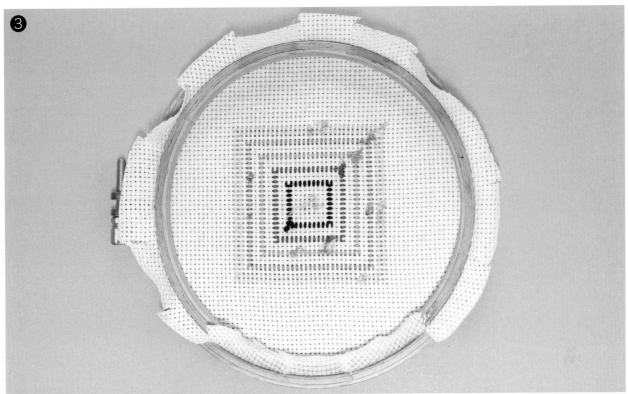

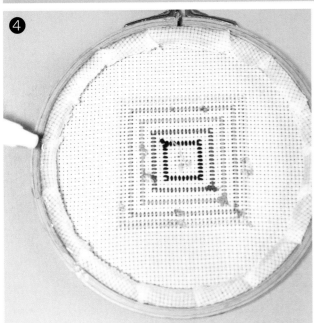

3. Fold the fabric over to glue it down.

4. Spread a new layer of glue on the outside ring and position the pre-cut back panel on top. Now turn the hoop over and hold for a few seconds. Let the finished design dry overnight while weighted down slightly.

5. This is what the back should look like!

FRECH
WILD
WUNDER
BAR

ANNA
&
BEN

PATTERNS

Page 27

Page 30

FLOWERS & WREATHS

This chapter is all about flowers—whether they're in wreaths, vases, or bouquets. Some designs can also make great ring pillows if you just add a silk ribbon for the rings.

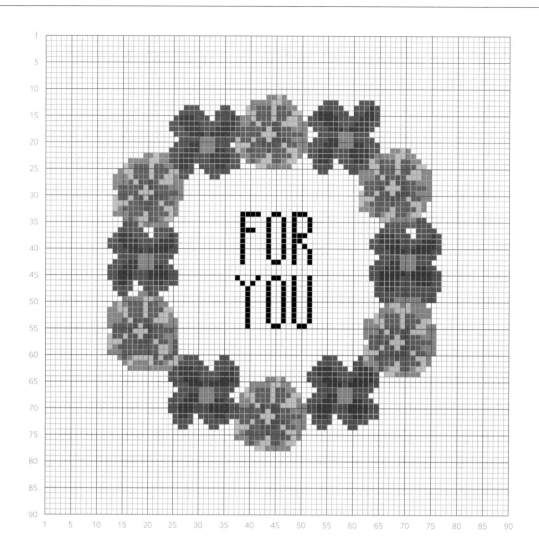

Difficulty: ✕ ✕ ✕

- ■ 122
- ■ 307
- ■ 308
- ▨ 311
- ■ 5975

☐ I would like to embroider this.

Embroidered on: _____

Gift for: _____

I used the following materials: _____

_____

_____

_____

_____

_____

Difficulty: ✗ ✗

- ■ 57
- ■ 109
- ■ 112
- ■ 205
- ■ 212
- ■ 306
- ■ 895
- ■ 972
- ■ 1017

Materials Used:

Hoop: 8″ (19cm)

Fabric: 14 count Aida (Perl-Aida 54 stitches / 10cm)

Fabric color: Cream

☐ I would like to embroider this.

Embroidered on: _____

Gift for: _____

I used the following materials: _____

_____

_____

_____

_____

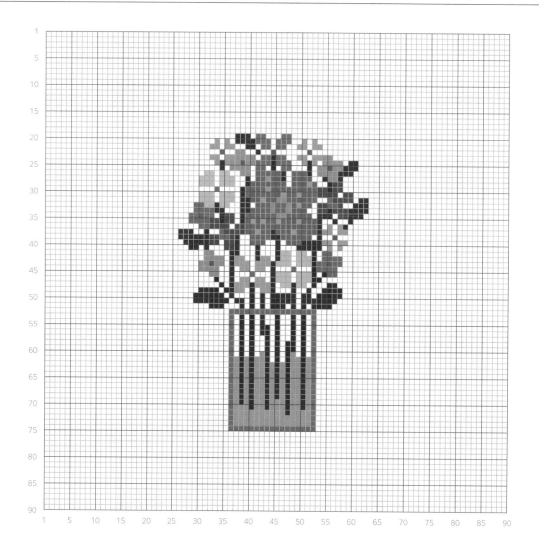

Difficulty: ✕✕

- ▨ 25
- ■ 39
- ■ 118
- ▨ 159
- ▨ 185
- ■ 230
- ■ 970
- ■ 1074
- ▨ 1017

☐ I would like to embroider this.

Embroidered on: _____

Gift for: _____

I used the following materials: _____
_____
_____
_____
_____
_____

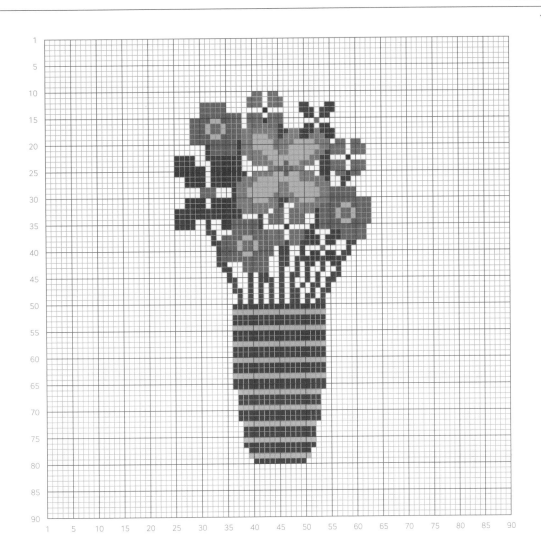

Difficulty: ✗ ✗

■ 10	■ 308
■ 89	■ 311
■ 121	■ 877
■ 142	■ 970
■ 306	

☐ I would like to embroider this.

Embroidered on: _____

Gift for: _____

I used the following materials: _____

_____

_____

_____

_____

_____

Difficulty: ✕✕

Motif 1

- 49
- 89
- 130
- 140
- 143
- 205
- 328
- 403
- 868
- 875
- 878
- 944
- 969

Motif 2

- 20
- 47
- 142
- 301
- 306
- 308
- 340
- 403
- 1012
- 5975

Motif 3

- 49
- 131
- 403
- 205
- 306
- 308
- 328
- 355
- 875
- 878
- 1017
- 1023

Materials Used (Motif 3):

Hoop: 7″ (16cm)

Fabric: 11 count Aida (Perl-Aida 44 stitches / 10cm)

Fabric color: Cream

Difficulty: ✕ ✕ ✕

- ☐ 001
- ■ 10
- ■ 47
- ■ 145
- ■ 208
- ■ 212
- ▨ 298
- ■ 307
- ■ 5975

☐ I would like to embroider this.

Embroidered on: _____

Gift for: _____

I used the following materials: _____

_____

_____

_____

_____

_____

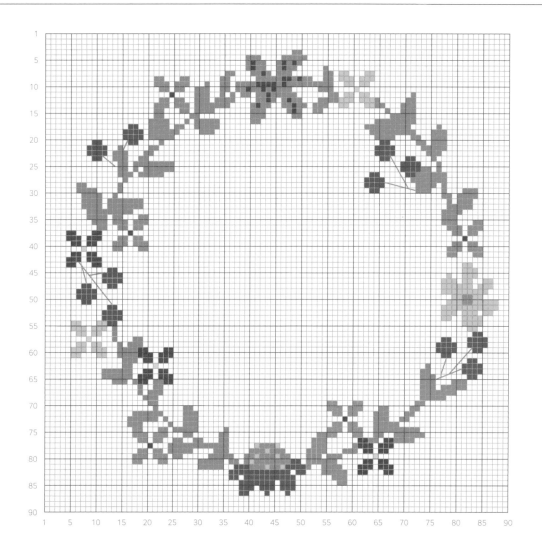

Difficulty: ✕✕

- ■ 47
- ■ 74
- ■ 108
- ■ 131
- ■ 208
- ■ 306

☐ I would like to embroider this.

Embroidered on: _____

Gift for: _____

I used the following materials: _____

_____

_____

_____

_____

_____

✕✕

Difficulty: ✗✗

- 49
- 60
- 298
- 328
- 69
- 969
- 860

☐ I would like to embroider this.

Embroidered on: _____

Gift for: _____

I used the following materials: _____

_____

_____

_____

_____

_____

Difficulty: ✗✗

- ■ 210
- ■ 308
- ■ 295
- ■ 316
- ■ 302
- ■ 5975

☐ I would like to embroider this.

Embroidered on: _____

Gift for: _____

I used the following materials: _____
_____
_____
_____
_____
_____

Difficulty: ✕✕

▨	49	▨	298
■	89	▨	328
■	205	▨	1017

☐ I would like to embroider this.

Embroidered on: _____

Gift for: _____

I used the following materials: _____

_____

_____

_____

_____

_____

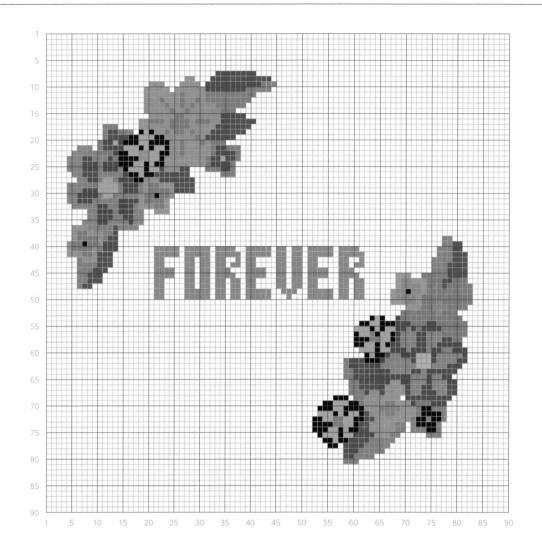

Difficulty: ✕ ✕

- ▨ 108
- ■ 134
- ▨ 185
- ▨ 188
- ▨ 306
- ▨ 307
- ▨ 779
- ■ 860
- ▨ 875
- ▨ 895

☐ I would like to embroider this.

Embroidered on: _____

Gift for: _____

I used the following materials: _____

_____

_____

_____

_____

_____

Difficulty: ✗ ✗ ✗

- 49
- 204
- 306
- 307
- 896
- 1016
- 1023

☐ I would like to embroider this.

Embroidered on: _____

Gift for: _____

I used the following materials: _____

_____

_____

_____

_____

_____

Page 52

Page 40

Page 51

LETTERS & SAYINGS

Here you will find some funny, encouraging, and beautiful sayings, as well as an embroidery alphabet that you can use to create your own designs. This chapter also contains a 3-D alphabet decorated with geometric patterns.

Difficulty: ✕

- ■ 118
- ■ 328
- ■ 186
- ■ 895
- ■ 298

Materials Used:

Hoop: 8″ (19cm)

Fabric: 11 count Aida (Perl-Aida 44 stitches / 10cm)

Fabric color: Cream

☐ I would like to embroider this.

Embroidered on: _____

Gift for: _____

I used the following materials: _____

_____
_____
_____
_____
_____

Difficulty: ✕

■ 109   ■ 298
■ 131   ■ 330
■ 204   ■ 9046

☐ I would like to embroider this.

Embroidered on: _____

Gift for: _____

I used the following materials: _____

_____

_____

_____

_____

_____

Difficulty: ✕

- ■ 134
- ■ 298

☐ I would like to embroider this.

Embroidered on: _____

Gift for: _____

I used the following materials: _____

_____

_____

_____

_____

_____

Difficulty: ✕✕

☐ 001
◼ 29
◼ 9046

☐ I would like to embroider this.

Embroidered on: _____

Gift for: _____

I used the following materials: _____

Difficulty: ✕

- ■ 118
- ■ 298
- ■ 328
- ■ 895

☐ I would like to embroider this.

Embroidered on: _____

Gift for: _____

I used the following materials: _____

_____

_____

_____

_____

_____

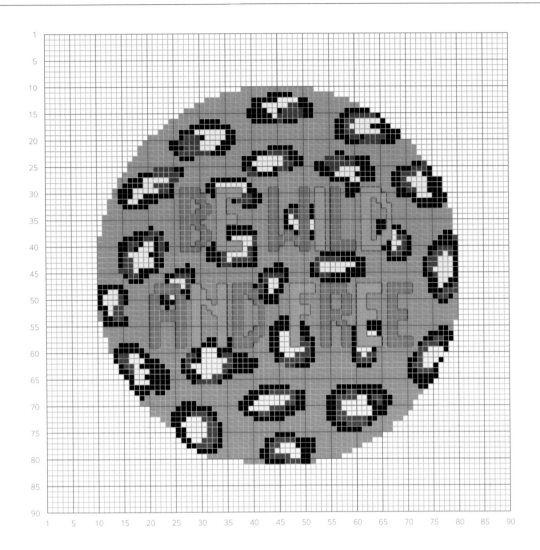

Difficulty: ✕ ✕ ✕

■ 109	■ 403
☐ 275	■ 944
■ 342	■ 1084

Tip:

I recommend you outline the letters with a black thread to make them stand out against the leopard-print background.

☐ I would like to embroider this.

Embroidered on: _____

Gift for: _____

I used the following materials: _____

_____

_____

_____

_____

Difficulty: ✕

- ■ 118
- ■ 133
- ■ 186
- ■ 298
- ■ 328
- ■ 403
- ■ 895

☐ I would like to embroider this.

Embroidered on: _____

Gift for: _____

I used the following materials: _____

_____

_____

_____

_____

_____

Difficulty: ✕

■ 20   ■ 403
■ 22   ■ 9046

☐ I would like to embroider this.

Embroidered on: _____

Gift for: _____

I used the following materials: _____

_____

_____

_____

_____

Motif 1

- 89
- 103
- 129
- 142
- 188
- 298
- 335

Motif 2

- 49
- 89
- 142
- 204
- 210
- 298
- 328

☐ I would like to embroider this.

Embroidered on: _____

Gift for: _____

I used the following materials: _____

_____

_____

_____

_____

_____

Difficulty: ✗ ✗ ✗

- 36
- 78
- 131
- 870
- 875
- 979
- 1028
- 1066
- 1074

Tip:

Use a marker to mark out the letters that will remain blank—this will serve as a guide. Then start with one flower, such as the pink one (Color 78), and embroider all the flowers of this color. Do this either flower by flower or color by color, and then finally fill the spaces in between.

☐ I would like to embroider this.

Embroidered on: _____

Gift for: _____

I used the following materials: _____

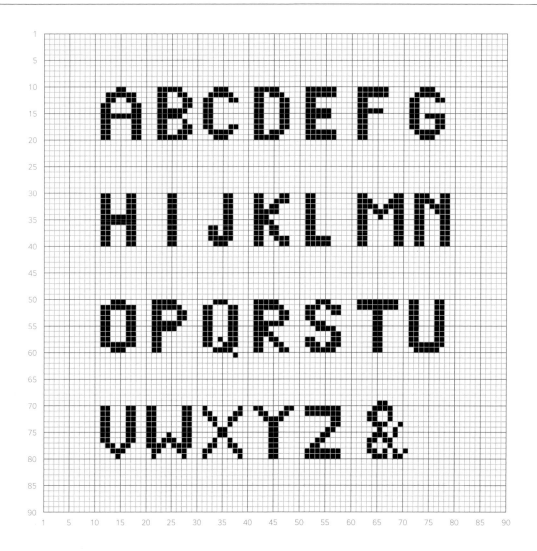

Difficulty: ✕

■ 403

☐ I would like to embroider this.

Embroidered on: _____

Gift for: _____

I used the following materials: _____

_____

_____

_____

_____

_____

Difficulty: ✗✗

☐ 001
■ 129
■ 131
■ 143
■ 145
■ 150
■ 1098

Materials Used:

Hoop: 8″ (19cm)

Fabric: 14 count Aida (Perl-Aida 54 stitches / 10cm)

Fabric color: White

Tip:

Outline the word "circus" with red thread to make it stand out better from the fabric.

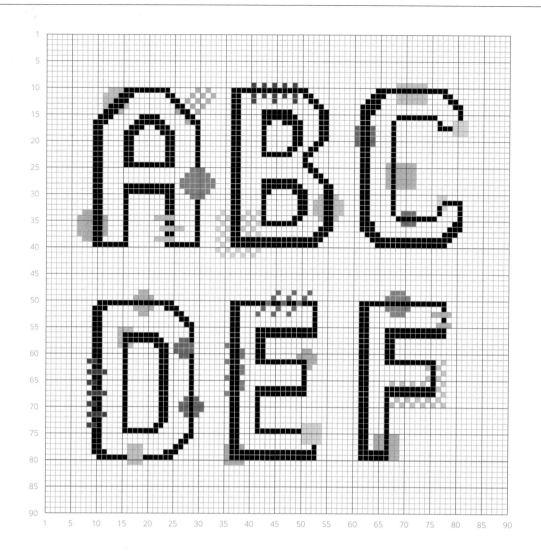

Difficulty: ✗

- 49
- 60
- 89
- 298
- 328
- 403
- 859

Materials Used:

Hoop: 5″ (13cm)

Fabric: 8 count Aida (Kilim-Aida 33 stitches / 10cm)

Fabric color: Off-white

☐ I would like to embroider this.

Embroidered on: _____

Gift for: _____

I used the following materials: _____

_____

_____

_____

_____

_____

Difficulty: ✕

▨ 49	▨ 328	
▨ 60	■ 403	
■ 89	▨ 859	
▨ 298		

☐ I would like to embroider this.

I used the following materials: _____

Embroidered on: _____

_____

Gift for: _____

_____

_____

_____

Difficulty: ✕

- ▪ 49
- ▪ 60
- ▪ 89
- ▪ 298
- ▪ 328
- ■ 403
- ▪ 859

☐ I would like to embroider this.

Embroidered on: _____

Gift for: _____

I used the following materials: _____

_____

_____

_____

_____

_____

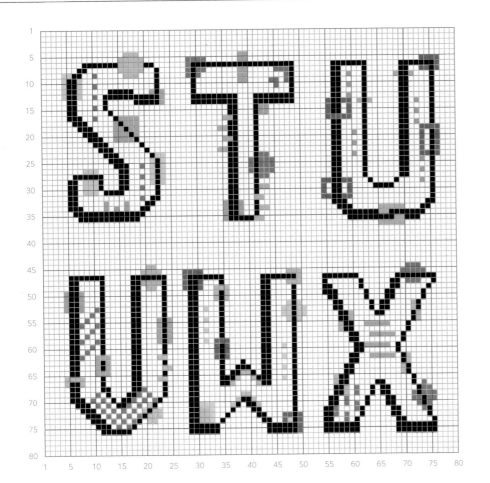

Difficulty: ✕

▪ 49	▪ 328
▪ 60	▪ 403
▪ 89	▪ 859
▪ 298	

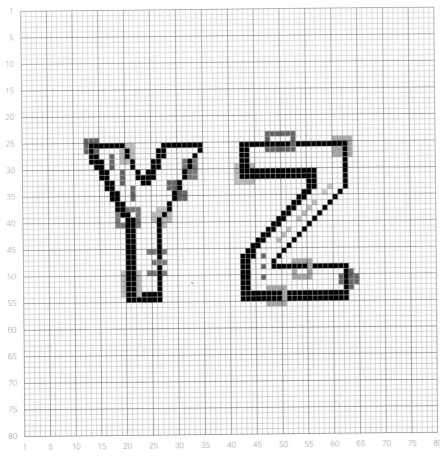

Difficulty: ✕

▪ 49	▪ 328
▪ 60	▪ 403
▪ 89	▪ 859
▪ 298	

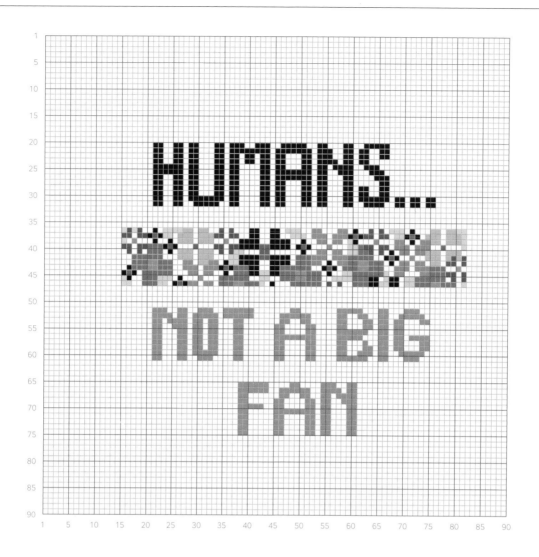

Difficulty: ✕✕

- ■ 29
- ■ 118
- ■ 129
- ■ 148
- ▨ 187
- ▨ 895
- ▨ 1092
- ■ 1066

☐ I would like to embroider this.

Embroidered on: _____

Gift for: _____

I used the following materials: _____

_____

_____

_____

_____

_____

Difficulty: ✗ ✗

- ☐ 001
- ■ 208
- ■ 210
- ■ 212
- ▨ 290
- ▨ 291
- ▨ 292
- ▨ 295
- ■ 9046

☐ I would like to embroider this.

Embroidered on: _____

Gift for: _____

I used the following materials: _____

_____

_____

_____

_____

_____

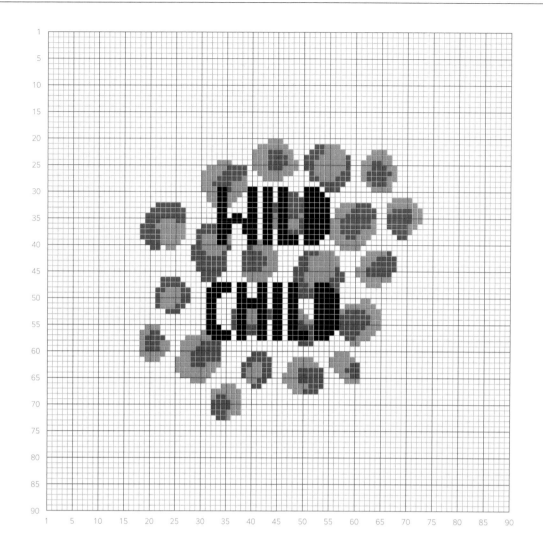

Difficulty: ✕ ✕

- ■ 59
- ■ 62
- ■ 403

Tip:

Start with the letters first. They will serve as a guide for the leopard-print pattern.

☐ I would like to embroider this.

Embroidered on: _____

Gift for: _____

I used the following materials: _____

_____

_____

_____

_____

_____

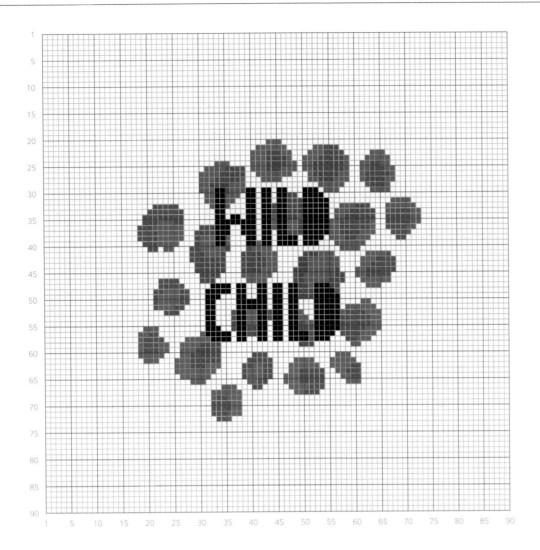

Difficulty: ✕✕

■ 59
■ 131
■ 403

☐ I would like to embroider this.

Embroidered on: _____

Gift for: _____

I used the following materials: _____

_____

_____

_____

_____

_____

Difficulty: ✗

- ■ 19
- ■ 60

☐ I would like to embroider this.

Embroidered on: _____

Gift for: _____

I used the following materials: _____

_____

_____

_____

_____

_____

Difficulty: ✗

◻ 292   ◼ 328
◼ 306   ◼ 895

Tip:

Embroider the letters first and the sun at the end.

◻ I would like to embroider this.

Embroidered on: _____

Gift for: _____

I used the following materials: _____

_____

_____

_____

_____

_____

Difficulty: ✕

- ■ 46
- ■ 118
- ■ 129
- ■ 139
- ■ 205
- ■ 230
- ■ 298
- ■ 333

☐ I would like to embroider this.

Embroidered on: _____

Gift for: _____

I used the following materials: _____

_____

_____

_____

_____

_____

Difficulty: ✕ ✕

- 109
- 209
- 306
- 403
- 970
- 972
- 1017

☐ I would like to embroider this.

Embroidered on: _____

Gift for: _____

I used the following materials: _____

Difficulty: ✕

- ■ 109
- ■ 403
- ■ 895

☐ I would like to embroider this.

Embroidered on: _____

Gift for: _____

I used the following materials: _____

_____

_____

_____

_____

_____

Difficulty: ✕✕

■ 109   ■ 328
■ 306   ■ 895

☐ I would like to embroider this.

Embroidered on: _____

Gift for: _____

I used the following materials: _____

_____

_____

_____

_____

_____

Page 68

NATURE & PLANTS

The plant world is very diverse, so it's a theme that definitely shouldn't be missing from a modern embroidery book. In addition to a monstera leaf, you will also find cacti, deciduous trees, and many other plants in this chapter.

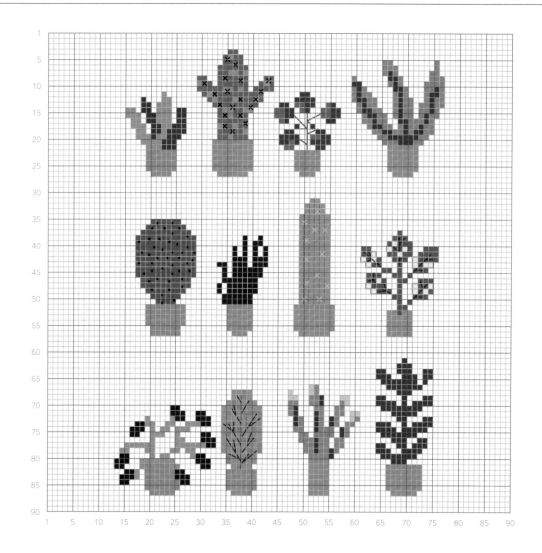

Difficulty: ✕

☐ 001　■ 311
■ 203　■ 859
■ 210　■ 878
■ 218　■ 923

Materials Used:

Hoop: 7″ (16cm)

Fabric: 11 count Aida (Perl-Aida 44 stitches / 10cm)

Fabric color: Cream

☐ I would like to embroider this.

Embroidered on: _____

Gift for: _____

I used the following materials: _____

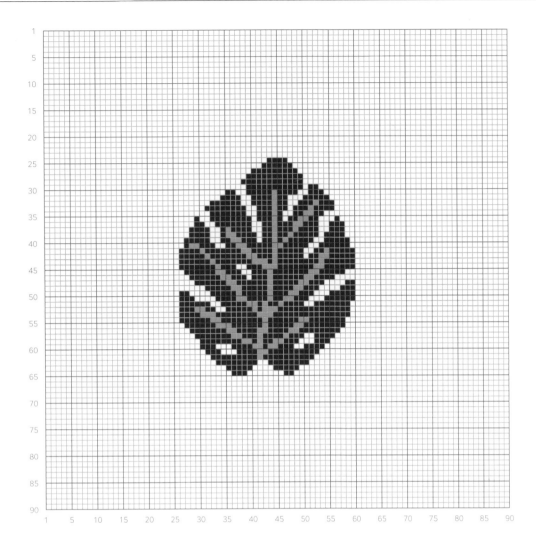

Difficulty: ✕

■ 203
■ 212

☐ I would like to embroider this.

Embroidered on: _____

Gift for: _____

I used the following materials: _____

_____

_____

_____

_____

_____

■ 47   ■ 338
■ 212   ■ 370
■ 313   ■ 403

☐ I would like to embroider this.

Embroidered on: _____

Gift for: _____

I used the following materials: _____

_____

_____

_____

_____

_____

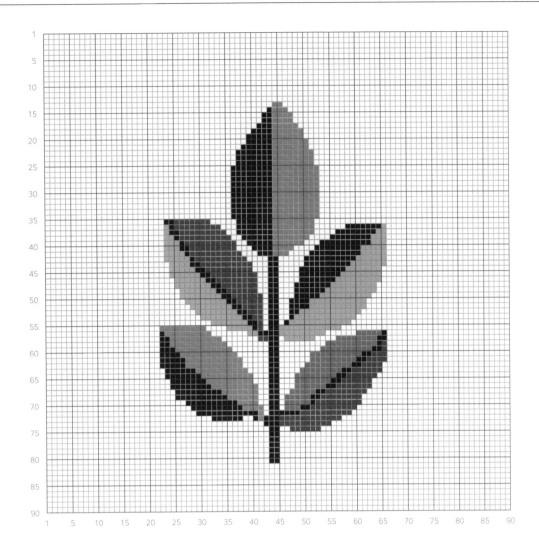

Difficulty: ✗ ✗

■ 47   ■ 338
■ 212   ■ 9575
■ 313

☐ I would like to embroider this.

Embroidered on: _____

Gift for: _____

I used the following materials: _____

_____

_____

_____

_____

_____

Difficulty: ✗ ✗ ✗

- ■ 47
- ■ 212
- ■ 313
- ■ 338
- ■ 875
- ■ 9575

☐ I would like to embroider this.

Embroidered on: _____

Gift for: _____

I used the following materials: _____

_____

_____

_____

_____

_____

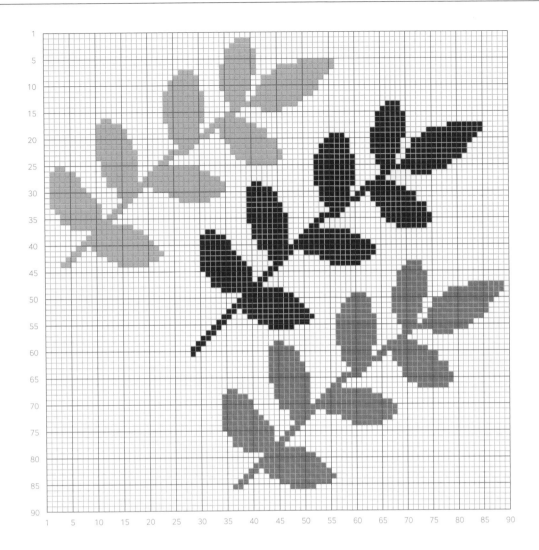

Difficulty: ✕ ✕

- ■ 212
- ■ 313
- ■ 338

☐ I would like to embroider this.

Embroidered on: _____

Gift for: _____

I used the following materials: _____

_____

_____

_____

_____

_____

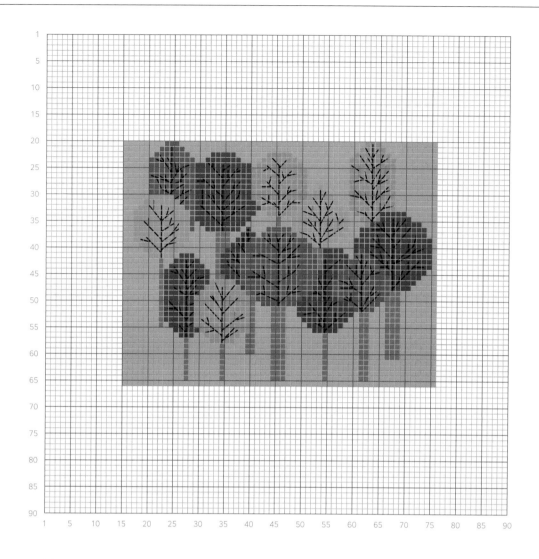

Difficulty: ✕ ✕

- ■ 122
- ■ 403
- ■ 185
- ■ 868
- ■ 189
- ■ 970
- ■ 369
- ■ 1017

☐ I would like to embroider this.

Embroidered on: _____

Gift for: _____

I used the following materials: _____

_____
_____
_____
_____
_____

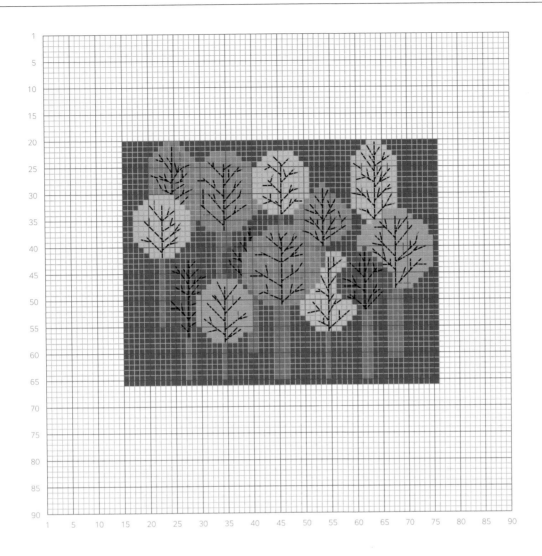

Difficulty: ✕✕

- ■ 210
- ■ 403
- ■ 307
- ■ 868
- ■ 311
- ■ 1003
- ■ 369

☐ I would like to embroider this.

Embroidered on: _____

Gift for: _____

I used the following materials: _____

_____

_____

_____

_____

_____

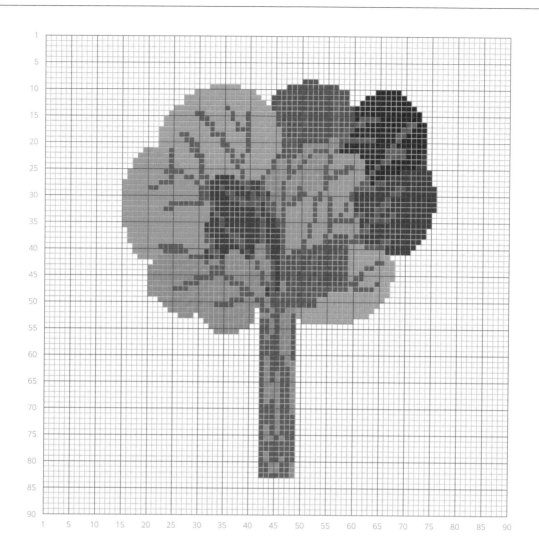

Difficulty: ✕✕

- ■ 122
- ■ 185
- ■ 189
- ■ 369
- ■ 868
- ■ 970
- ■ 1017
- ■ 1082

☐ I would like to embroider this.

Embroidered on: _____

Gift for: _____

I used the following materials: _____

_____

_____

_____

_____

_____

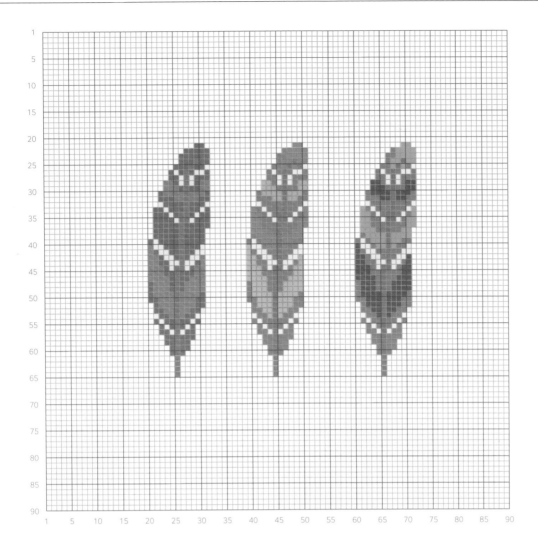

Difficulty: ✕✕

Feather 1

■ 121
□ 275
■ 882
■ 871
■ 1017

Feather 2

■ 203
□ 275
■ 298
■ 324
■ 882

Feather 3

□ 275
■ 858
■ 875
■ 882
■ 895

□ I would like to embroider this.

Embroidered on: _____

Gift for: _____

I used the following materials: _____
_____
_____
_____
_____
_____

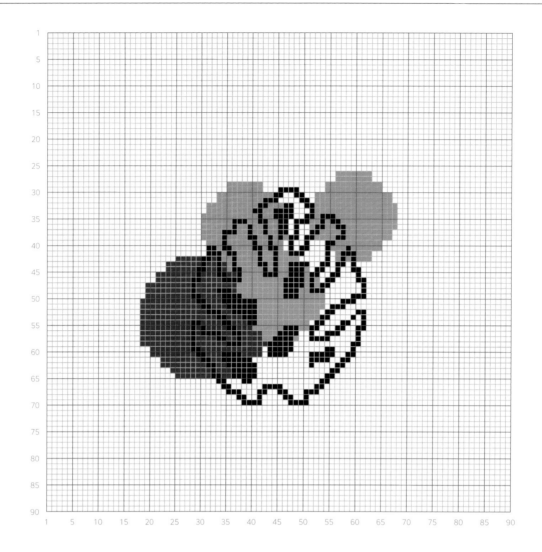

Difficulty: ✕✕

■ 230   ■ 895
■ 242   ■ 1084
■ 403

☐ I would like to embroider this.

Embroidered on: _____

Gift for: _____

I used the following materials: _____

_____

_____

_____

_____

_____

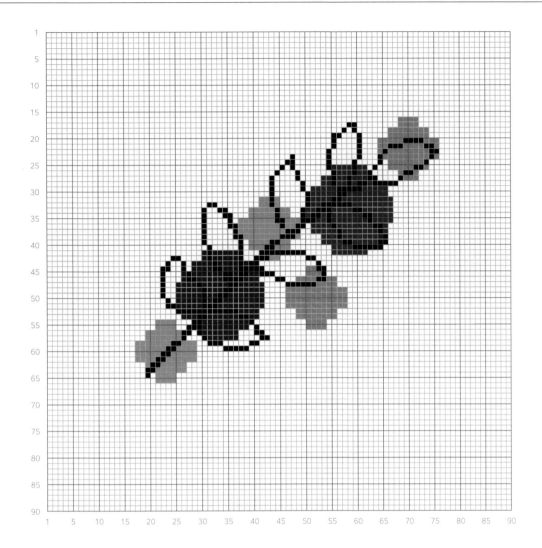

Difficulty: ✗ ✗

- ■ 208
- ■ 230
- ■ 403
- ■ 875
- ■ 877

☐ I would like to embroider this.

Embroidered on: _____

Gift for: _____

I used the following materials: _____

_____

_____

_____

_____

_____

Page 86

Page 91

CHILDREN'S BEDROOM

Rockets, animals, the solar system, colorful rain showers—all these can be found in this chapter. It's all about keeping things bright and fun for the little ones.

Difficulty: ✕✕

- ■ 11
- ■ 298
- ■ 204
- ■ 306
- ■ 230
- ■ 403
- ■ 231
- ■ 868

☐ I would like to embroider this.

Embroidered on: _____

Gift for: _____

I used the following materials: _____
_____
_____
_____
_____
_____

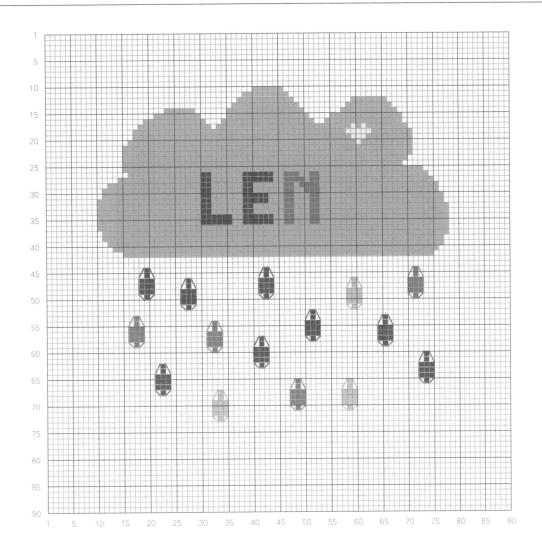

Difficulty: ✕

- ■ 29
- ■ 129
- ■ 131
- ■ 188
- ■ 298

Tip:

Personalize the cloud
with a name, and then
use it as a door sign
for a child's room.

☐ I would like to embroider this.

Embroidered on: _____

Gift for: _____

I used the following materials: _____

_____

_____

_____

_____

Difficulty: ✗✗

■	11	■	298
■	20	■	326
■	47	■	339
■	148	■	367
■	162	■	890
■	185	■	914
■	212	■	977
■	231	■	1014

Tip:

Counted fabric is available in many different colors.

This means you can give your image a certain look. The motif can still be stitched on white fabric in any case.

☐ I would like to embroider this.

Embroidered on: _____

Gift for: _____

I used the following materials: _____

_____

_____

_____

_____

_____

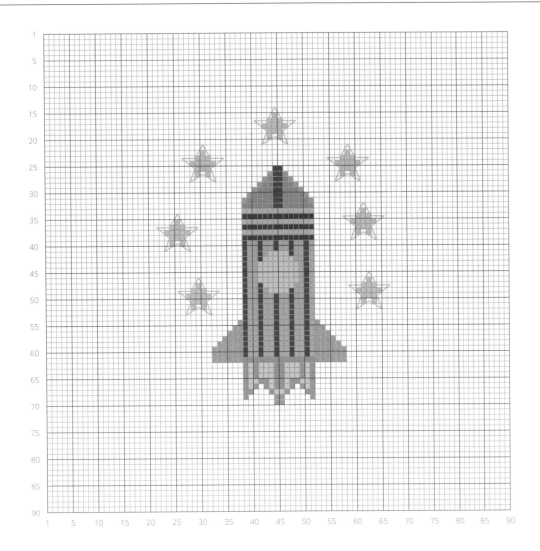

Difficulty: ✕

- ■ 10
- ■ 47
- ■ 162
- ■ 298
- ■ 302
- ■ 326
- ■ 328
- ■ 398

☐ I would like to embroider this.

Embroidered on: _____

Gift for: _____

I used the following materials: _____

_____

_____

_____

_____

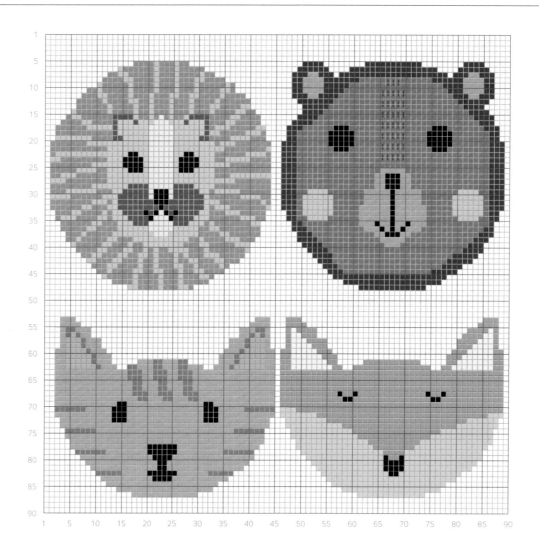

Difficulty: ✕✕

Lion

- ■ 306
- ■ 360
- ■ 386
- ■ 403
- ■ 891

Bear

- ■ 48
- ■ 347
- ■ 357
- ■ 403
- ■ 1007

Cat

- ■ 234
- ■ 328
- ■ 399
- ■ 403

Fox

- □ 001
- ■ 326
- ■ 403
- ■ 933

Materials Used (Lion):

Hoop: 5″ (13cm)

Fabric: 14 count Aida (Perl-Aida 54 stitches / 10cm)

Fabric color: White

Difficulty: ✕✕

■ 36	■ 188
■ 62	■ 298
■ 109	■ 328
■ 117	■ 360
■ 119	■ 379

☐ I would like to embroider this.

Embroidered on: _____

Gift for: _____

I used the following materials: _____

_____

_____

_____

_____

_____

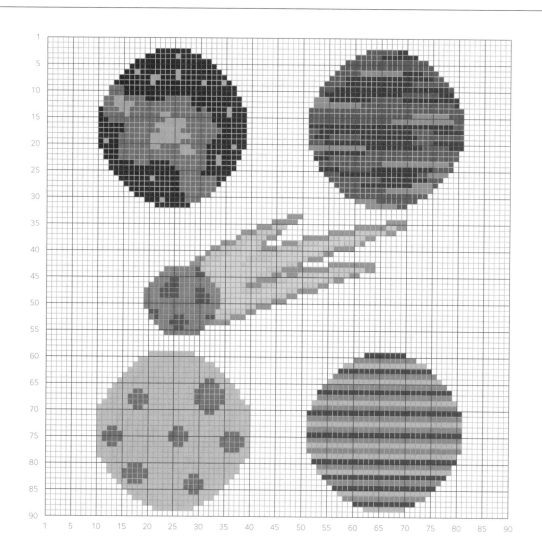

Difficulty: ×

Mercury
- 234
- 235
- 400

Venus
- 326
- 339
- 1014

Comet
- 290
- 298
- 333
- 326
- 1014

Moon
- 234
- 235

Uranus
- 129
- 162
- 169

☐ I would like to embroider this.

Embroidered on: _____

Gift for: _____

I used the following materials: _____

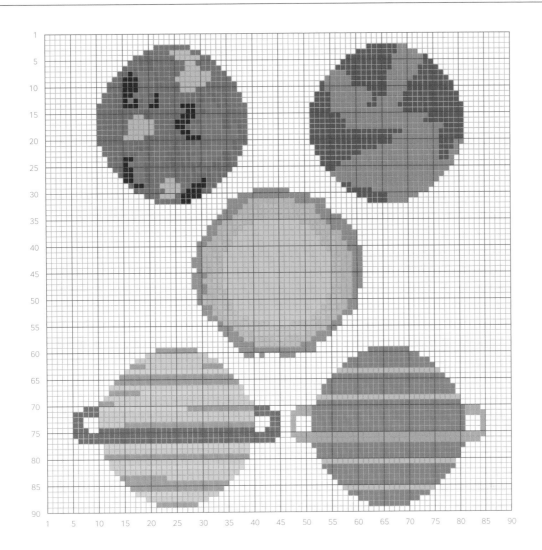

Difficulty: ✕

Earth
- 129
- 146
- 212
- 243
- xxx

Mars
- 339
- 326

Sun
- 290
- 298
- 306
- 326

Saturn
- 292
- 305
- 1007
- 1084

Neptune
- 121
- 186
- 1092

Tip:

The individual planets can be stitched in small embroidery hoops and spread out across the wall.

Difficulty: ✕ ✕

☐ 001   ■ 230

■ 19   ■ 403

■ 208   ■ 5975

☐ I would like to embroider this.

Embroidered on: _____

Gift for: _____

I used the following materials: _____

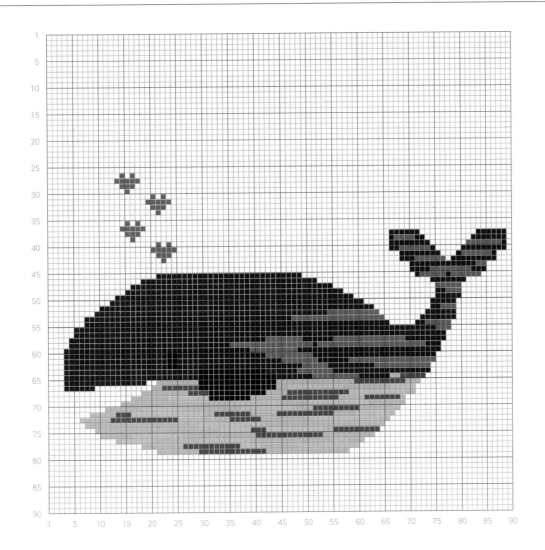

Difficulty: ✕ ✕

▨	120	■	403
■	131	■	779
■	134	▨	1092
■	150	■	9046

Materials Used:

Hoop: 8″ (19cm)

Fabric: 14 count Aida (Perl-Aida 55 stitches / 10cm)

Fabric color: Light blue

☐ I would like to embroider this.

Embroidered on: _____

Gift for: _____

I used the following materials: _____

_____

_____

_____

_____

_____

Page 98

FOOD & KITCHEN

In this chapter, you'll find motifs that are appropriate to the theme, such as lots of fruit and vegetables but also a colorful ice cream or two.

Difficulty: ✕✕

Row 1

(from left to right)

- ■ 111
- ■ 169
- ■ 238
- ■ 298
- ■ 313
- ■ 326
- ■ 379
- ■ 879
- ■ 870
- ■ 1027

Row 2

- ■ 10
- ■ 19
- ■ 187
- ■ 246
- ■ 162
- ■ 206
- ■ 313
- ■ 238
- ■ 328
- ■ 379

Row 3

- ■ 19
- ■ 76
- ■ 78
- ■ 90
- ■ 206
- ■ 208
- ■ 246
- □ 275
- ■ 313
- ■ 403

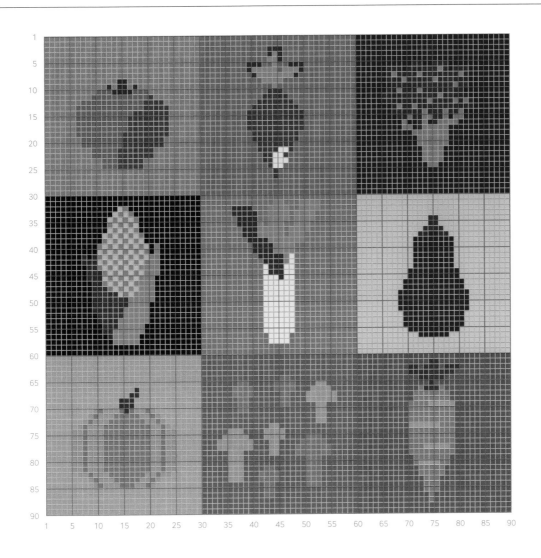

Difficulty: ✕✕

Row 1
(from left to right)

- 20
- 43
- 47
- 70
- 208
- 212
- 226
- 275
- 308
- 1076

Row 2

- 70
- 134
- 212
- 226
- 275
- 298
- 308
- 333

Row 3

- 169
- 212
- 328
- 333
- 376
- 870
- 970
- 1007

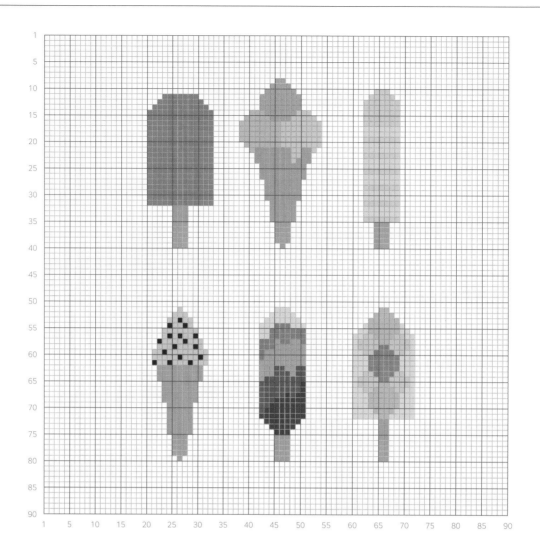

Difficulty: ✕

■ 49		■ 305	
■ 62		■ 328	
■ 63		■ 358	
■ 89		■ 888	
■ 298			

☐ I would like to embroider this.

Embroidered on: _____

Gift for: _____

I used the following materials: _____

_____

_____

_____

_____

_____

_____

Difficulty: ✕

- ■ 28
- ■ 29
- ■ 291
- ■ 302
- ■ 316
- ■ 323
- ■ 328
- ■ 888

☐ I would like to embroider this.

Embroidered on: _____

Gift for: _____

I used the following materials: _____

_____

_____

_____

_____

_____

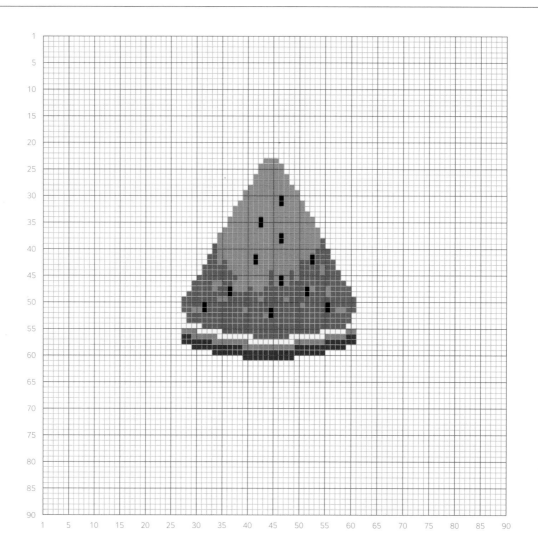

Difficulty: ✕

- ■ 76
- ■ 78
- ■ 208
- ■ 212
- ☐ 275
- ■ 403

Materials Used:

Hoop: 4″ (10.5cm)

Fabric: 14 count Aida (Perl-Aida 54 stitches / 10cm)

Fabric color: White

☐ I would like to embroider this.

Embroidered on: _____

Gift for: _____

I used the following materials: _____

_____

_____

_____

_____

_____

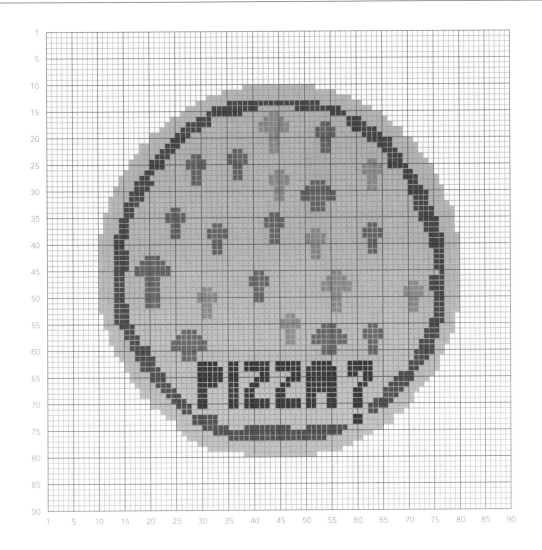

Difficulty: ✕ ✕

- ■ 13
- ▨ 305
- ■ 47
- ■ 376
- ▨ 298
- ■ 870

☐ I would like to embroider this.

Embroidered on: _____

Gift for: _____

I used the following materials: _____

_____

_____

_____

_____

Page 103

GEOMETRIC ANIMALS

Animals made of geometric patterns are very popular, and so they simply had to feature in this book. From simple and natural to colorful and playful, there's something for everyone. The level of difficulty is a little higher in this chapter, but the end result is worth the effort.

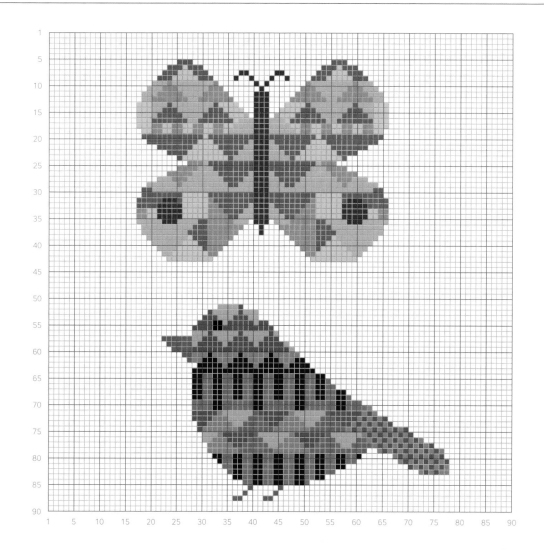

Difficulty: ✗ ✗ ✗

Bird

- ■ 121
- ■ 150
- ■ 186
- ■ 189
- ■ 403
- ■ 923
- ■ 978
- ■ 5975

Butterfly

- ■ 70
- ■ 74
- ■ 89
- ■ 291
- ■ 306

☐ I would like to embroider this.

Embroidered on: _____

Gift for: _____

I used the following materials: _____

_____

_____

_____

_____

_____

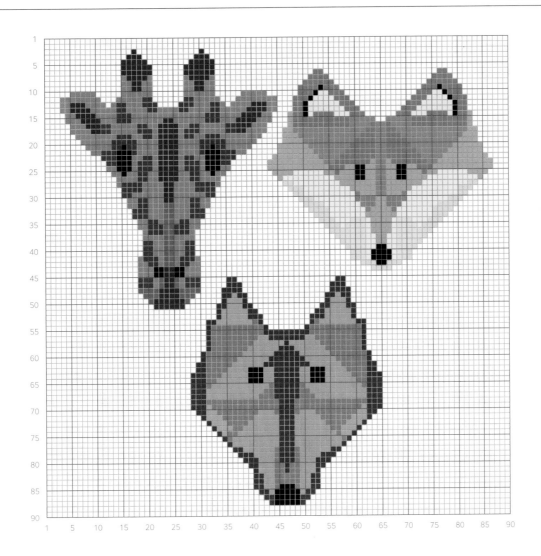

Difficulty: × × ×

Giraffe
- ■ 310
- ▨ 307
- ▨ 308
- ■ 403
- ▨ 1014

Fox
- ☐ 001
- ▨ 300
- ▨ 308
- ▨ 330
- ▨ 361
- ■ 403
- ▨ 1003
- ▨ 1048

Wolf
- ▨ 232
- ▨ 235
- ■ 400
- ■ 403
- ▨ 9575

Materials Used (Fox):

Hoop: 4˝ (10.5cm)

Fabric: 14 count Aida (Perl-Aida 54 stitches / 10cm)

Fabric color: White

☐ I would like to embroider this.

Embroidered on: _____

Gift for: _____

I used the following materials: _____

_____

_____

_____

_____

_____

Page 115

Page 114

Page 116

ABSTRACT ART

Squares, circles, triangles—inside, outside,
overlapping one another. Anything goes in this
chapter. The abstract images come in "sets of
four" but also look great as a single design.

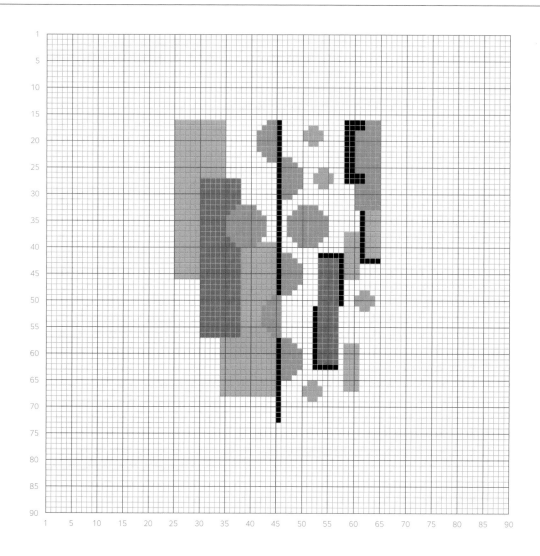

Difficulty: ✕ ✕

- 328
- 398
- 399
- 403
- 870

☐ I would like to embroider this.

Embroidered on: _____

Gift for: _____

I used the following materials: _____

_____

_____

_____

_____

_____

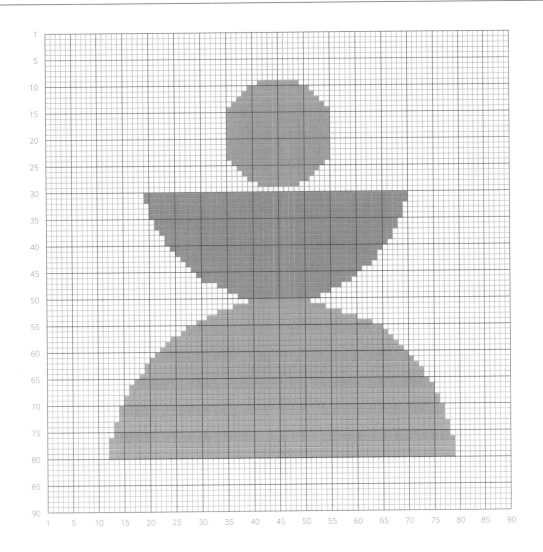

Difficulty: ✕ ✕

■ 328
■ 398
■ 870

☐ I would like to embroider this.

Embroidered on: _____

Gift for: _____

I used the following materials: _____

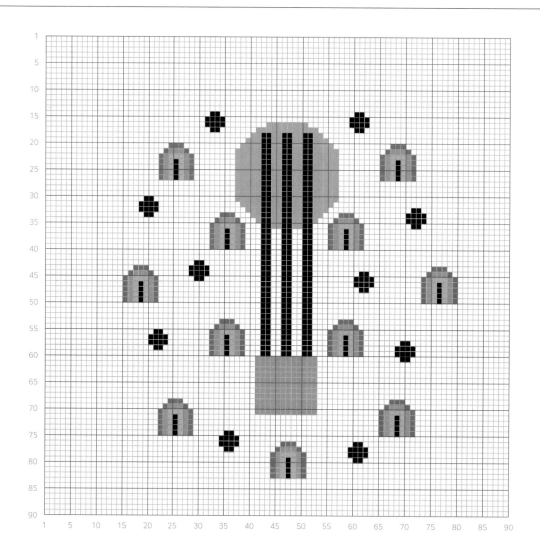

Difficulty: ✕✕

- ■ 328
- ■ 403
- ■ 398
- ■ 870
- ■ 399

☐ I would like to embroider this.

Embroidered on: _____

Gift for: _____

I used the following materials: _____

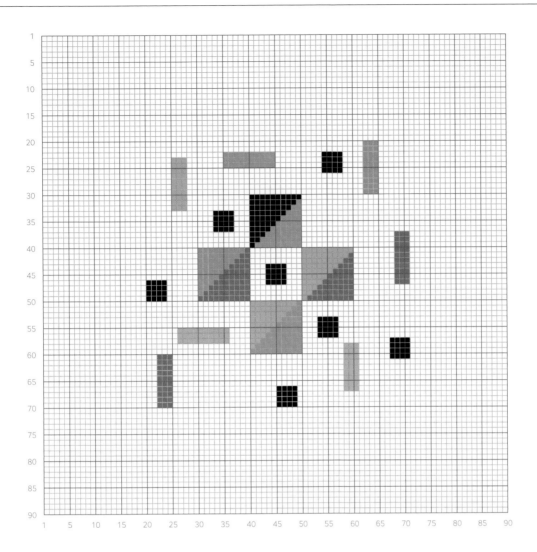

Difficulty: ✕✕

- 328
- 403
- 399
- 870

☐ I would like to embroider this.

Embroidered on: _____

Gift for: _____

I used the following materials: _____

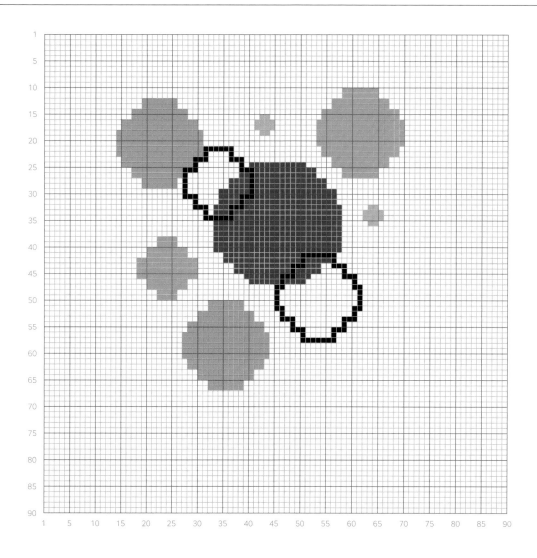

Difficulty: ✗

▨ 305 ■ 403

▨ 326 ■ 1014

▨ 337

☐ I would like to embroider this.

Embroidered on: _____

Gift for: _____

I used the following materials: _____

_____

_____

_____

_____

_____

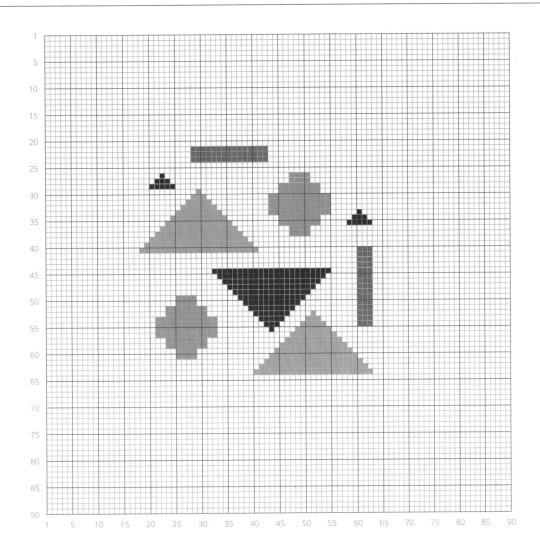

Difficulty: ✕

- ■ 305
- ■ 326
- ■ 337
- ■ 1014

☐ I would like to embroider this.

Embroidered on: _____

Gift for: _____

I used the following materials: _____

_____

_____

_____

_____

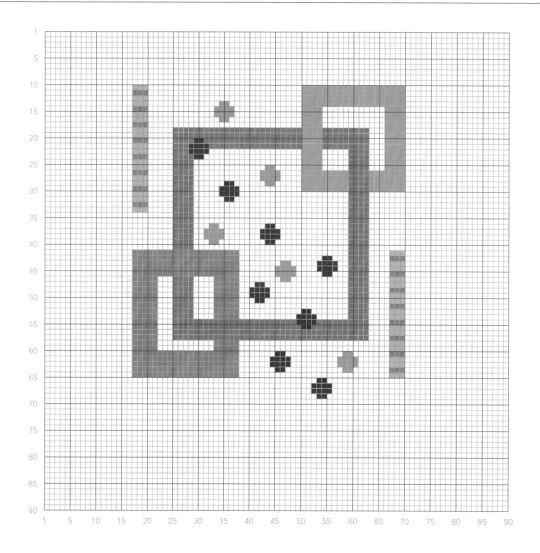

Difficulty: ✕

■ 307 ■ 337
■ 326 ■ 338
■ 328 ■ 1014

☐ I would like to embroider this.

Embroidered on: _____

Gift for: _____

I used the following materials: _____

_____

_____

_____

_____

_____

_____

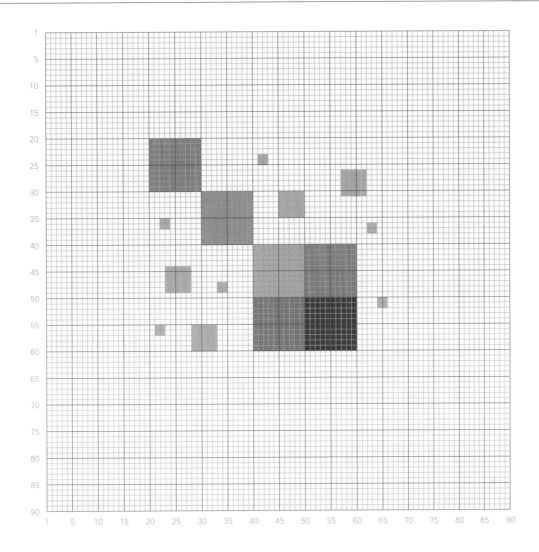

Difficulty: ✕✕

- ▩ 305
- ▩ 307
- ▩ 326
- ▩ 328
- ▩ 338
- ▩ 1014

☐ I would like to embroider this.

Embroidered on: _____

Gift for: _____

I used the following materials: _____

_____

_____

_____

_____

_____

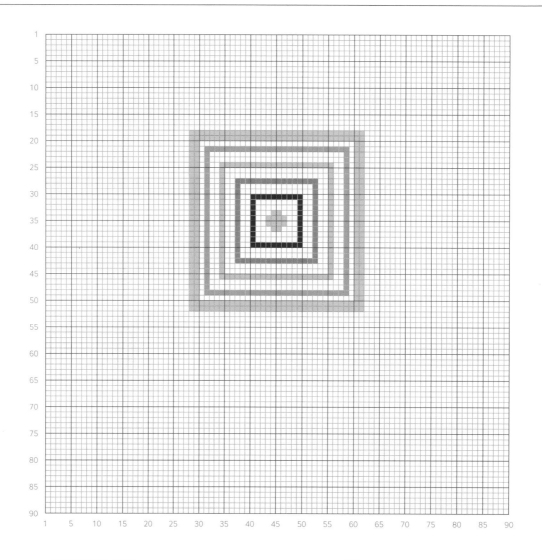

■ 72
■ 306
■ 870
▨ 893
■ 970

Materials Used:

Hoop: 5˝ (13cm)

Fabric: 14 count Aida (Perl-Aida 54 stitches / 10cm)

Fabric color: White

☐ I would like to embroider this.

Embroidered on: _____

Gift for: _____

I used the following materials: _____

_____

_____

_____

_____

_____

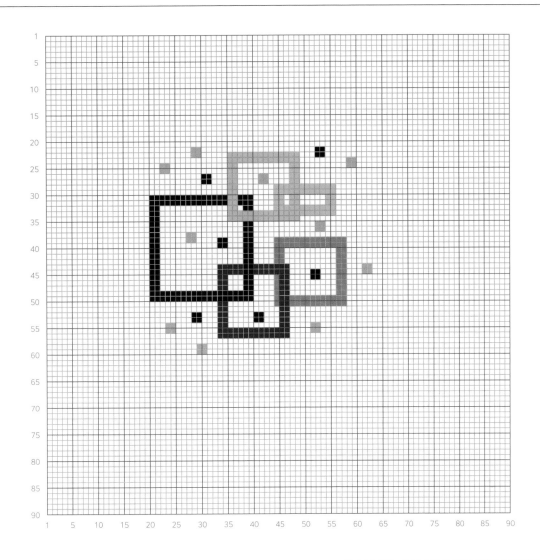

Difficulty: ✕

- ■ 72
- ■ 403
- ■ 306
- ▦ 893
- ■ 399
- ■ 970

Materials Used:

Hoop: 5˝ (13cm)

Fabric: 14 count Aida (Perl-Aida 54 stitches / 10cm)

Fabric color: White

☐ I would like to embroider this.

Embroidered on: _____

Gift for: _____

I used the following materials: _____

_____

_____

_____

_____

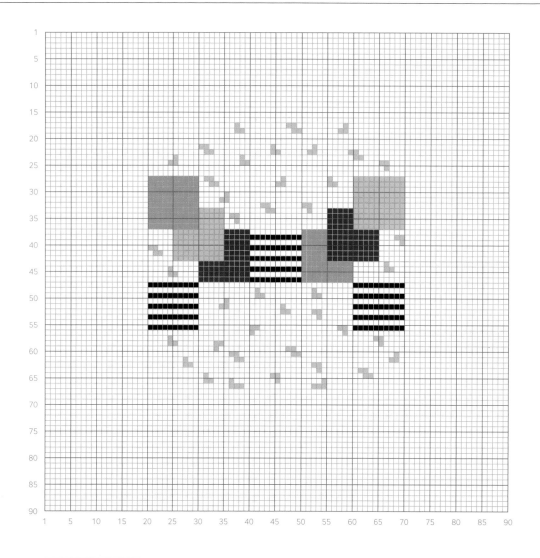

Materials Used:

Hoop: 5″ (13cm)

Fabric: 14 count Aida (Perl-Aida 54 stitches / 10cm)

Fabric color: White

☐ I would like to embroider this.

Embroidered on: _____

Gift for: _____

I used the following materials: _____

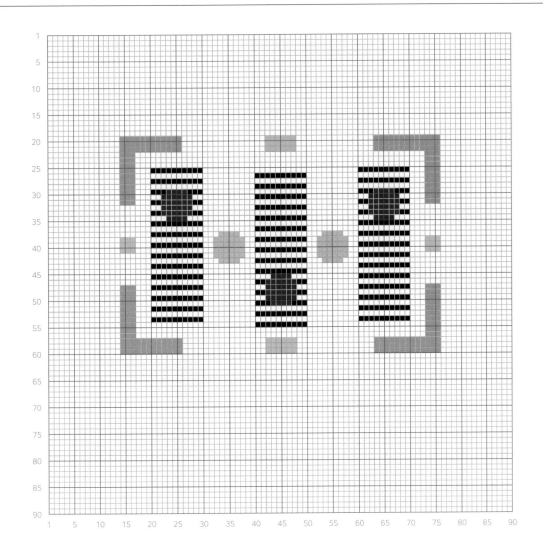

Difficulty: ✕ ✕

- ■ 72
- ■ 306
- □ 403
- ■ 870
- ■ 893

☐ I would like to embroider this.

Embroidered on: _____

Gift for: _____

I used the following materials: _____

_____

_____

_____

_____

_____

Page 120

COLORS & SHAPES

The title speaks for itself. Here you will find a selection of delicate color gradients and motifs that blend into one another. But there's also a brightly colored mix of shapes and some abstract rainbows.

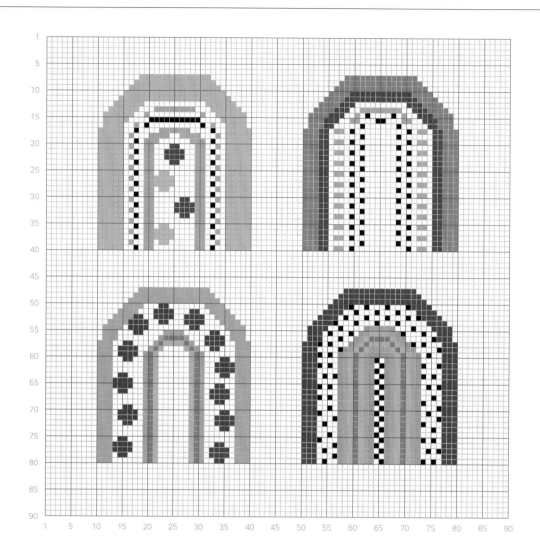

Top Row

- 305
- 328
- 337
- 378
- 403
- 1014

- 338
- 378
- 403
- 1014

Bottom Row

- 305
- 324
- 337
- 378
- 1014

- 305
- 324
- 337
- 338
- 403
- 1014

Materials Used (top right):

Hoop: 5″ (13cm)

Fabric: 14 count Aida (Perl-Aida 54 stitches / 10cm)

Fabric color: White

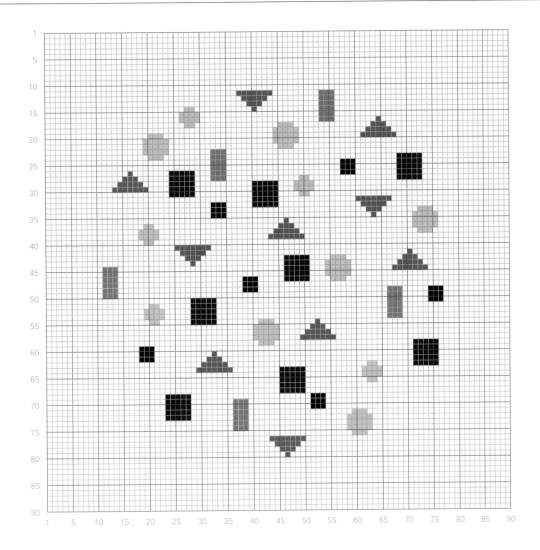

Difficulty: ✕

■ 47   ■ 338
■ 134   ■ 403
■ 298

☐ I would like to embroider this.   I used the following materials: _____

Embroidered on: _____

Gift for: _____

✕ ✕

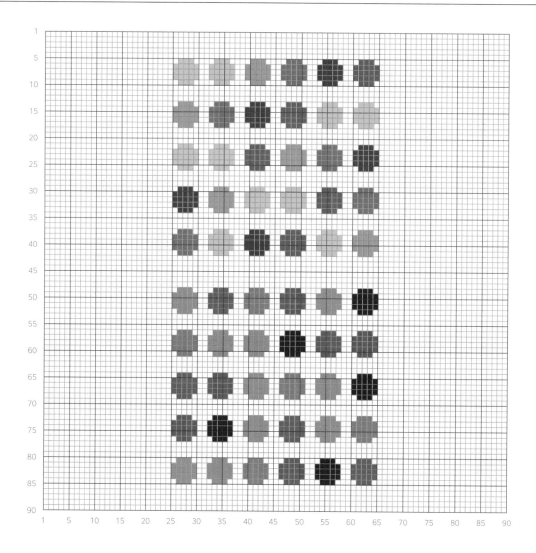

Difficulty: ✕ ✕

- ■ 13
- ■ 36
- ■ 97
- ■ 111
- ■ 134
- ■ 215
- ■ 217
- ■ 306
- ■ 341
- ■ 883
- ■ 1024
- ■ 1039

☐ I would like to embroider this.

Embroidered on: _____

Gift for: _____

I used the following materials: _____

_____

_____

_____

_____

_____

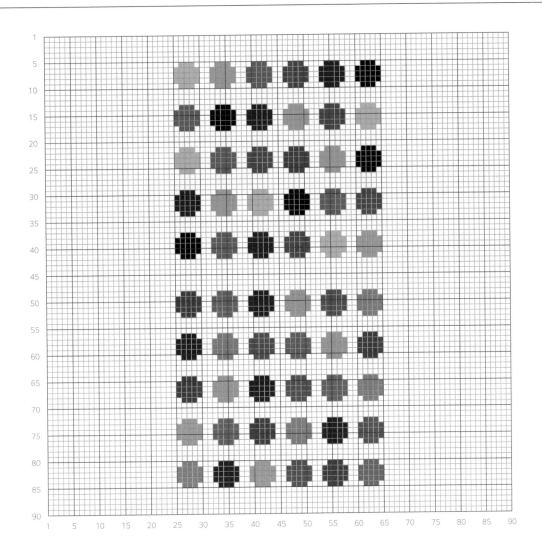

Difficulty: ✕ ✕

- 62
- 63
- 70
- 86
- 89
- 94
- 117
- 119
- 139
- 150
- 185
- 189

☐ I would like to embroider this.

Embroidered on: _____

Gift for: _____

I used the following materials: _____

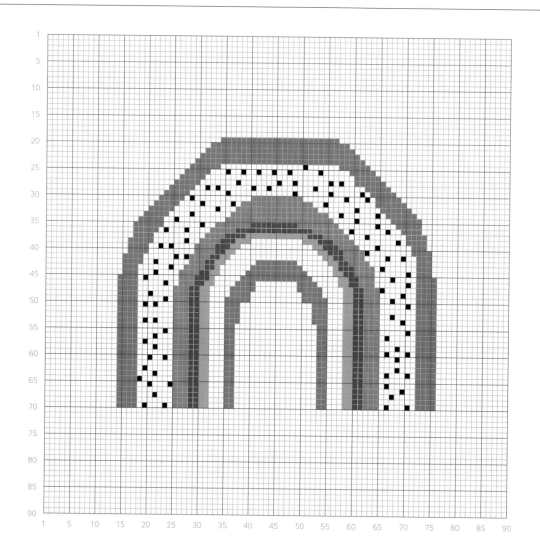

Difficulty: ✕

■ 185 ■ 969
■ 188 ■ 970
■ 403

☐ I would like to embroider this.

Embroidered on: _____

Gift for: _____

I used the following materials: _____

_____

_____

_____

_____

_____

✕ ✕

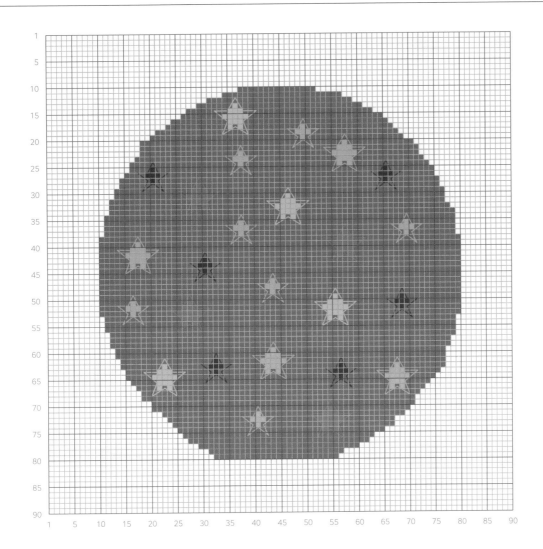

Difficulty: ✕ ✕

■ 118   ■ 306
■ 132   ■ 1023
■ 185

☐ I would like to embroider this.

Embroidered on: _____

Gift for: _____

I used the following materials: _____

_____

_____

_____

_____

_____

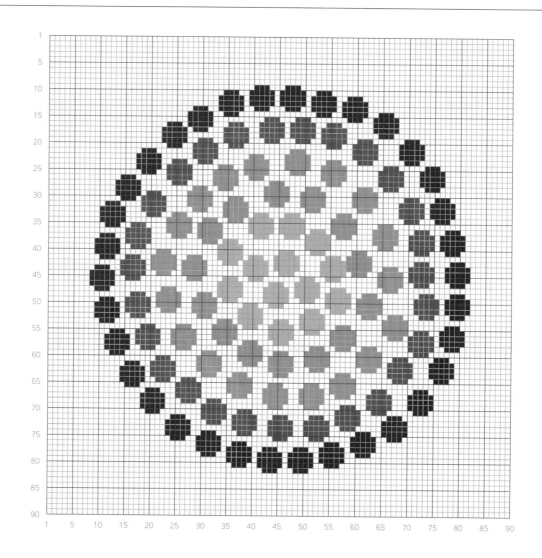

Difficulty: ✕✕

▪ 9	▪ 969
▪ 70	▪ 1027
▪ 895	

☐ I would like to embroider this.

Embroidered on: _____

Gift for: _____

I used the following materials: _____

_____

_____

_____

_____

_____

✕ ✕

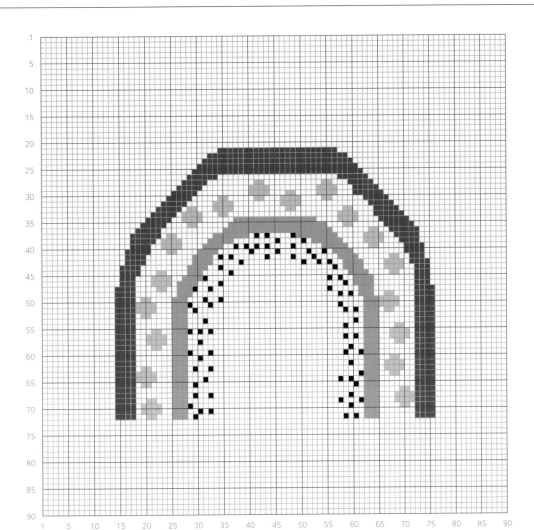

Difficulty: ✕

- ■ 185
- ■ 403
- ■ 968
- ■ 970

☐ I would like to embroider this.

Embroidered on: _____

Gift for: _____

I used the following materials: _____

_____

_____

_____

_____

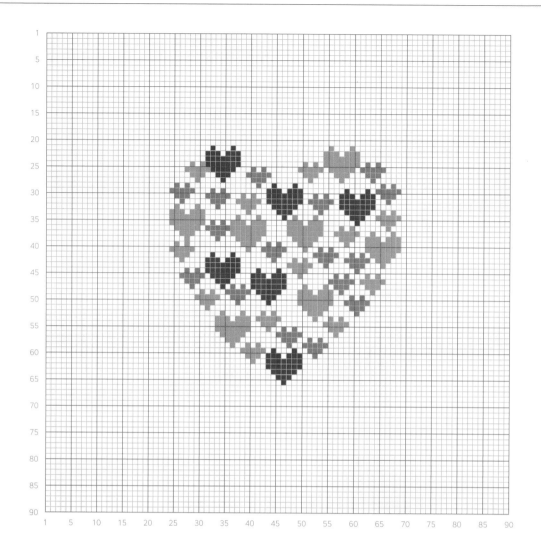

Difficulty: ✗✗

- ■ 76
- ■ 970
- ■ 972
- ■ 1017

☐ I would like to embroider this.

Embroidered on: _____

Gift for: _____

I used the following materials: _____

_____

_____

_____

_____

_____

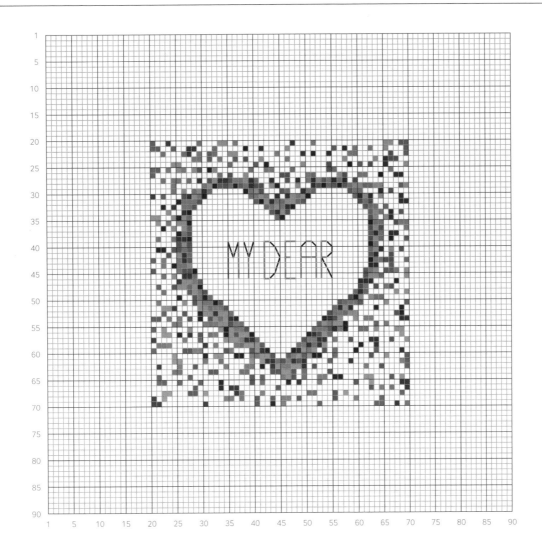

Difficulty: ✕

■ 20   ■ 110
■ 29   ■ 132
■ 76   ■ 895
■ 109

☐ I would like to embroider this.

Embroidered on: _____

Gift for: _____

I used the following materials: _____

_____

_____

_____

_____

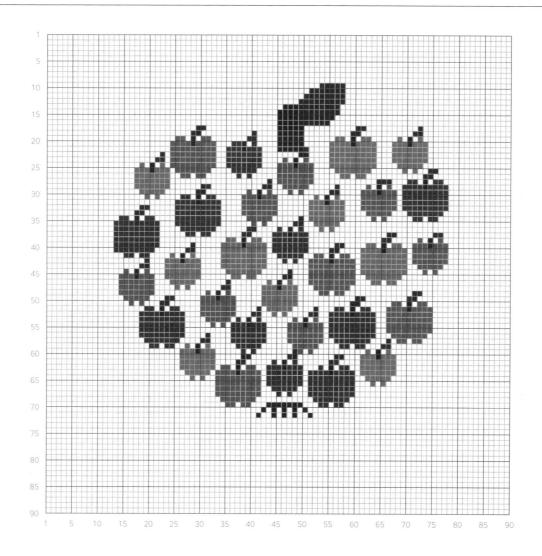

Difficulty: ✕✕✕

- ■ 11
- ■ 46
- ■ 230
- ■ 358
- ■ 1098

☐ I would like to embroider this.

Embroidered on: _____

Gift for: _____

I used the following materials: _____

_____

_____

_____

_____

_____

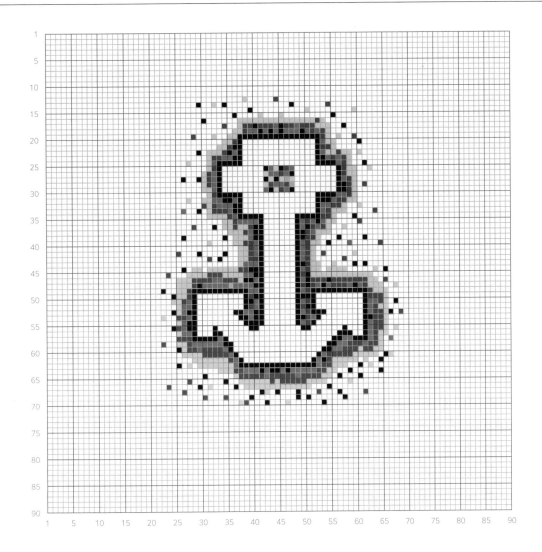

Difficulty: ✗

◻ 120   ◼ 137
◼ 134   ◼ 146

◻ I would like to embroider this.

Embroidered on: _____

Gift for: _____

I used the following materials: _____

Page 136

TRADITIONAL DESIGNS

This chapter is inspired by classic traditional designs from folk art. It includes Russian dolls in three different sizes and mirrored motifs in deep shades of red, blue, green, and yellow.

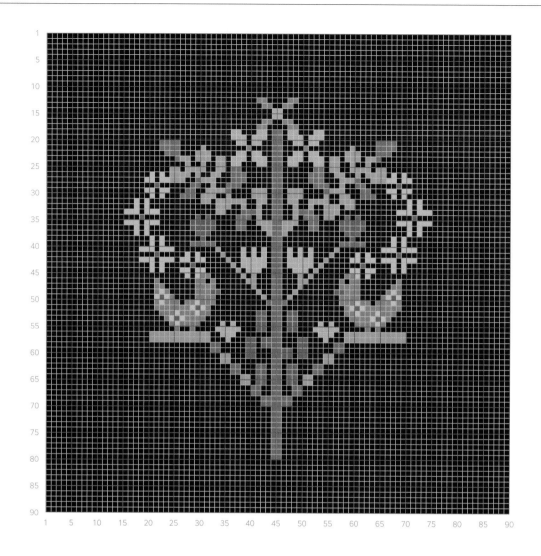

Difficulty: ✕ ✕

- ■ 47
- ■ 203
- ■ 298
- ■ 338
- ■ 860
- ▨ 1016
- ■ 1023

☐ I would like to embroider this.

Embroidered on: _____

Gift for: _____

I used the following materials: _____

Difficulty: ✕✕

☐ 001	■ 1014
■ 47	■ 1023
■ 187	■ 1066
■ 298	

Tip:

If you're embroidering the design onto a light-colored fabric, be sure to make the white flowers a little darker.

☐ I would like to embroider this.

Embroidered on: _____

Gift for: _____

I used the following materials: _____

_____

_____

_____

_____

_____

Difficulty: ✕✕

Motif 1

- ☐ 001
- ■ 39
- ■ 47
- ■ 306
- ■ 338
- ■ 403
- ■ 922

Motif 2

- ☐ 001
- ■ 11
- ■ 39
- ■ 47
- ■ 306
- ■ 336
- ■ 338
- ■ 403
- ■ 875
- ■ 921

Motif 3

- ☐ 001
- ■ 11
- ■ 39
- ■ 47
- ■ 149
- ■ 306
- ■ 338
- ■ 403
- ■ 921

Materials Used:

Fabric: 8 count Aida (Kilim-Aida 33 stitches / 10cm)

Fabric color: Off-white

Motif 1:
Hoop: 8˝ (19cm)

Motif 2:
Hoop: 7˝ (16cm)

Motif 3:
Hoop: 5˝ (13cm)

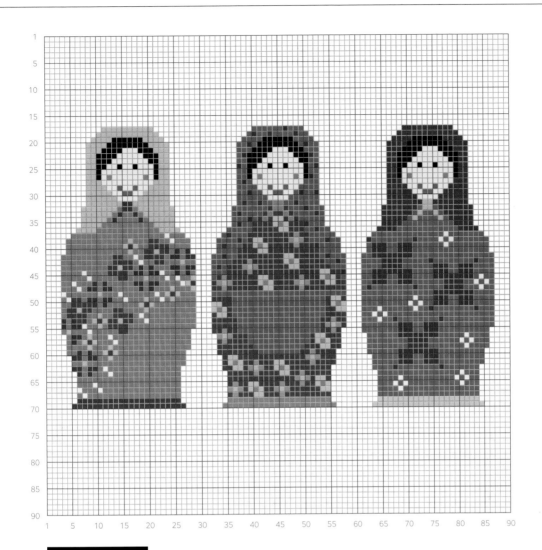

Difficulty: ✕✕

Motif 1

- ☐ 001
- ▪ 11
- ◼ 47
- ▫ 298
- ▪ 338
- ◼ 403
- ▪ 922
- ▪ 1076

Motif 2

- ▪ 11
- ▪ 47
- ▫ 298
- ▫ 305
- ▪ 326
- ▪ 338
- ◼ 403
- ▪ 922
- ◼ 1076
- ◼ 5957

Motif 3

- ☐ 001
- ▪ 11
- ◼ 47
- ▫ 298
- ◼ 403
- ▪ 922

☐ I would like to embroider this.

Embroidered on: _____

Gift for: _____

I used the following materials: _____

_____

_____

_____

_____

_____

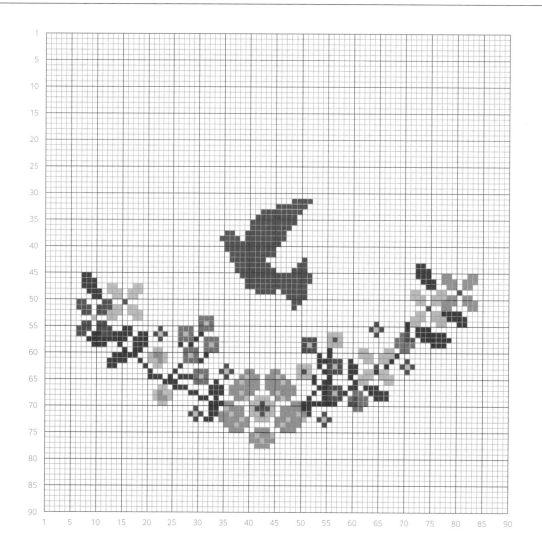

Difficulty: ✕✕

- ■ 13
- ■ 311
- ■ 324
- ■ 921
- ■ 1014
- ■ 1023
- ■ 1066

☐ I would like to embroider this.

Embroidered on: _____

Gift for: _____

I used the following materials: _____

_____

_____

_____

_____

_____

_____

✕ ✕

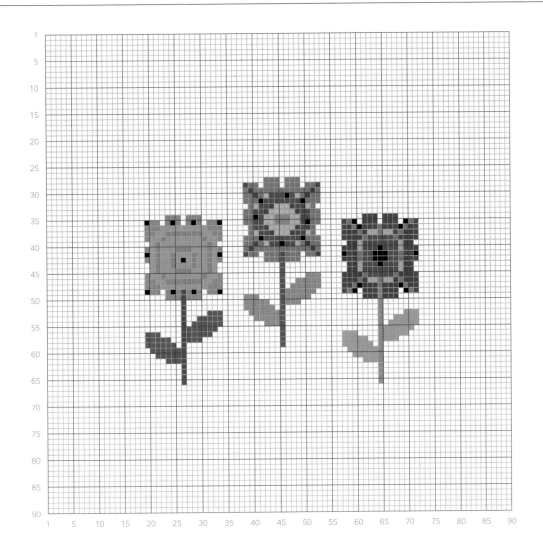

Difficulty: ✕

Flower 1

- ■ 47
- ■ 185
- ■ 189
- ■ 330
- ■ 403

Flower 2

- ■ 47
- ■ 189
- ■ 298
- ■ 330
- ■ 403
- ■ 1023

Flower 3

- ■ 47
- ■ 185
- ■ 189
- ■ 313
- ■ 330
- ■ 403
- ■ 1023

☐ I would like to embroider this.

Embroidered on: _____

Gift for: _____

I used the following materials: _____

_____

_____

_____

_____

_____

Page 146

Page 147

SEASONS & HOLIDAYS

In this chapter, we welcome spring, summer, fall, and winter with lots of little motifs that create one bigger design. The focus is slightly more on winter because of the holiday designs, with wintry wreaths, cozy candles, pretty Christmas tree ornaments, and winter landscapes. These offer so much potential when it comes to making your own Christmas gifts!

Difficulty: ✕ ✕

☐	001	■	203
■	9	■	298
■	10	■	306
■	11	■	9159

☐ I would like to embroider this.

Embroidered on: _____

Gift for: _____

I used the following materials: _____

_____

_____

_____

_____

_____

_____

Difficulty: ✕ ✕ ✕

- ■ 47
- ■ 212
- ■ 301
- ■ 403
- ■ 876

☐ I would like to embroider this.

Embroidered on: _____

Gift for: _____

I used the following materials: _____

_____

_____

_____

_____

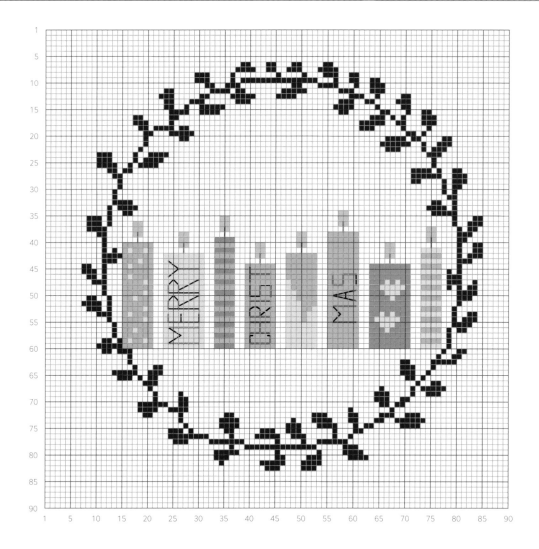

Difficulty: ✕ ✕ ✕

- ■ 29
- ■ 49
- ■ 75
- ■ 301
- ■ 403
- ■ 923

☐ I would like to embroider this.

Embroidered on: _____

Gift for: _____

I used the following materials: _____

_____

_____

_____

_____

_____

✕ ✕

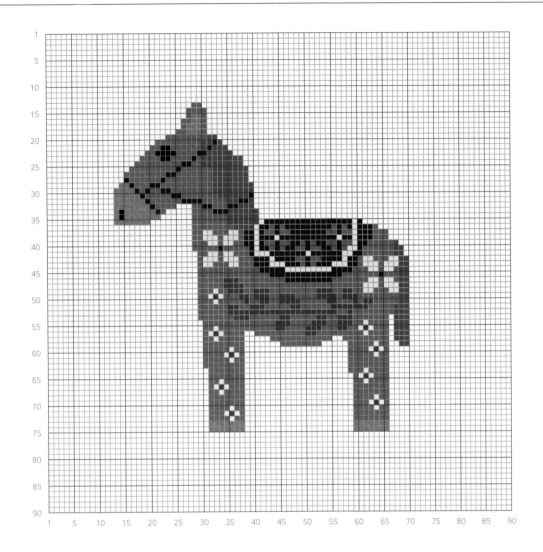

Difficulty: ✕ ✕

☐ 001   ■ 188
■ 47   ■ 338
■ 143   ■ 403
■ 134

☐ I would like to embroider this.

Embroidered on: _____

Gift for: _____

I used the following materials: _____
_____
_____
_____
_____
_____

✕✕

Difficulty: ✗ ✗

- ■ 137
- ■ 246
- ■ 306
- ■ 355
- ■ 369
- ■ 403
- ■ 848
- ■ 892
- ■ 923
- ■ 969
- ■ 1084

Materials Used:

Hoop: 9″ (22cm)

Fabric: 8 count Aida (Kilim-Aida 33 stitches / 10cm)

Fabric color: Blue

☐ I would like to embroider this.

Embroidered on: _____

Gift for: _____

I used the following materials: _____

Difficulty: ✕

- 47
- 203
- 205
- 218

Materials Used:

Hoop: 8″ (19cm)

Fabric: 11 count Aida (Perl-Aida 44 stitches / 10cm)

Fabric color: Cream

☐ I would like to embroider this.

Embroidered on: _____

Gift for: _____

I used the following materials: _____

_____

_____

_____

_____

Difficulty: ✗ ✗

- ■ 48
- ■ 206
- ■ 212
- ■ 229
- ■ 298
- ■ 307
- ■ 882
- ■ 969
- ■ 970

☐ I would like to embroider this.

Embroidered on: _____

Gift for: _____

I used the following materials: _____

_____

_____

_____

_____

_____

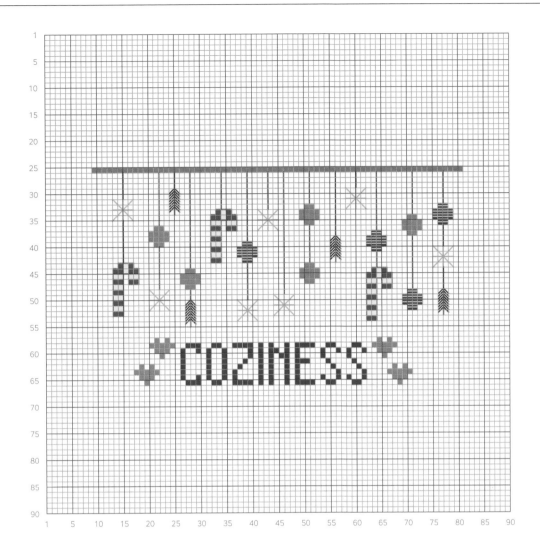

Difficulty: ✕✕

☐ 001	▨ 914
▨ 47	▨ 970
▨ 298	▨ 1017
▪ 403	▨ 5975
▨ 877	

☐ I would like to embroider this.

Embroidered on: _____

Gift for: _____

I used the following materials: _____

_____

_____

_____

_____

_____

Difficulty: ✕

☐ 001

Tip:

The snowflakes can be stitched in a small embroidery hoop and hung on the Christmas tree.

☐ I would like to embroider this.

Embroidered on: _____

Gift for: _____

I used the following materials: _____

Difficulty: ✕ ✕

- ■ 10
- ■ 22
- ■ 47
- ■ 210
- ■ 379
- ■ 878
- ■ 879

☐ I would like to embroider this.

Embroidered on: _____

Gift for: _____

I used the following materials: _____

_____

_____

_____

_____

_____

✕ ✕

Difficulty: ✕

Ornament 1
- 131
- 230
- 305
- 859

Ornament 2
- 49
- 131
- 298
- 403
- 972

Ornament 3
- 001
- 49
- 131

Tip:

The Christmas ornaments can be stitched in a small embroidery hoop and hung on the Christmas tree.

□ I would like to embroider this.

Embroidered on: _____

Gift for: _____

I used the following materials: _____

Difficulty: ×

Ornament 1

- ☐ 001
- ■ 19
- ■ 142
- ■ 301
- ■ 403

Ornament 2

- ☐ 001
- ■ 19
- ■ 47
- ■ 298
- ■ 301
- ■ 403

Ornament 3

- ■ 19
- ■ 203
- ■ 246
- ■ 298
- ■ 301
- ■ 403
- ■ 5975

☐ I would like to embroider this.

Embroidered on: _____

Gift for: _____

I used the following materials: _____

_____

_____

_____

_____

Difficulty: ✕✕

- ■ 29
- ■ 47
- ■ 49
- ■ 108
- ■ 121
- ■ 131
- ■ 298
- ■ 309
- ■ 311
- ■ 328
- ■ 335
- ■ 399
- ■ 403
- ■ 882
- ■ 923

☐ I would like to embroider this.

Embroidered on: _____

Gift for: _____

I used the following materials: _____

_____

_____

_____

_____

_____

Difficulty: ✕ ✕

- 🟫 29
- 🟫 47
- 🟩 129
- ⬛ 131
- ⬛ 132
- 🟫 210
- ⬜ 302
- 🟧 313
- 🟧 328
- 🟧 347
- ⬛ 403
- 🟥 1082

☐ I would like to embroider this.

Embroidered on: _____

Gift for: _____

I used the following materials: _____

_____

_____

_____

_____

Difficulty: ✕✕

- ☐ 001
- ■ 10
- ■ 47
- ■ 215
- ■ 298
- ■ 324
- ■ 326
- ■ 351
- ■ 358
- ■ 370
- ■ 378
- ■ 403
- ■ 877
- ■ 978
- ■ 1003
- ■ 1014
- ■ 1048
- ■ 1076

☐ I would like to embroider this.

Embroidered on: _____

Gift for: _____

I used the following materials: _____

_____

_____

_____

_____

_____

Difficulty: ✕ ✕

□ 001	■ 779	
■ 10	■ 848	
■ 47	■ 850	
■ 244	■ 851	
■ 302	■ 903	
■ 314	■ 977	
■ 403		

□ I would like to embroider this.

Embroidered on: _____

Gift for: _____

I used the following materials: _____

_____

_____

_____

_____

_____

MY OWN DESIGNS

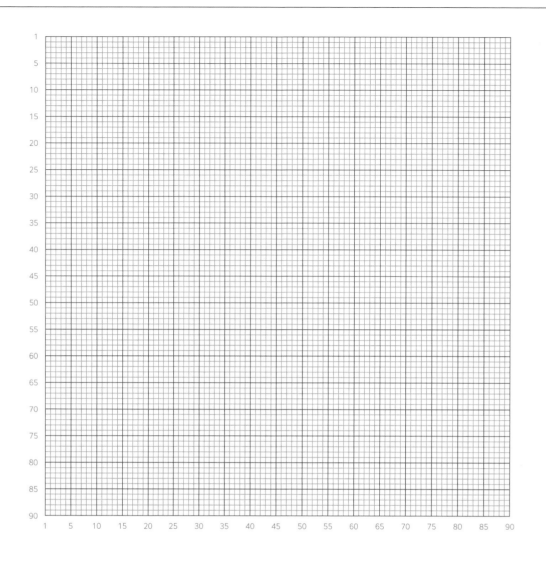

My thread colors:

☐ ☐ ☐ ☐
☐ ☐ ☐ ☐
☐ ☐ ☐ ☐
☐ ☐ ☐ ☐
☐ ☐ ☐ ☐
☐ ☐ ☐ ☐
☐ ☐ ☐ ☐

☐ I would like to embroider this.

Embroidered on: _____

Gift for: _____

I used the following materials: _____

_____

_____

_____

_____

_____

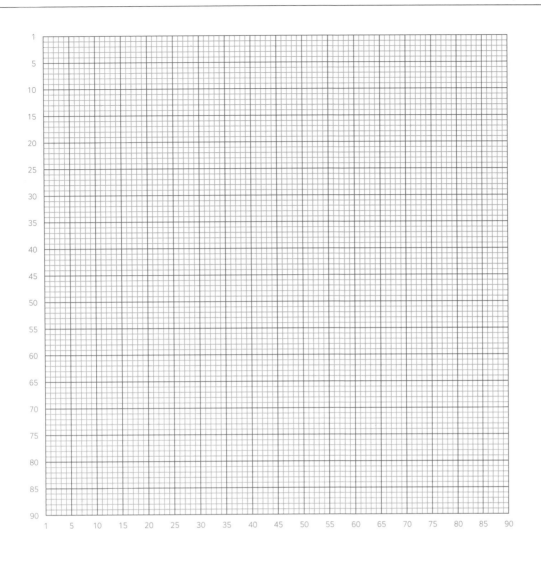

My thread colors:

☐ ☐ ☐ ☐
☐ ☐ ☐ ☐
☐ ☐ ☐ ☐
☐ ☐ ☐ ☐
☐ ☐ ☐ ☐
☐ ☐ ☐ ☐
☐ ☐ ☐ ☐

☐ I would like to embroider this.

Embroidered on: _____

Gift for: _____

I used the following materials: _____

_____

_____

_____

_____

_____

× ×

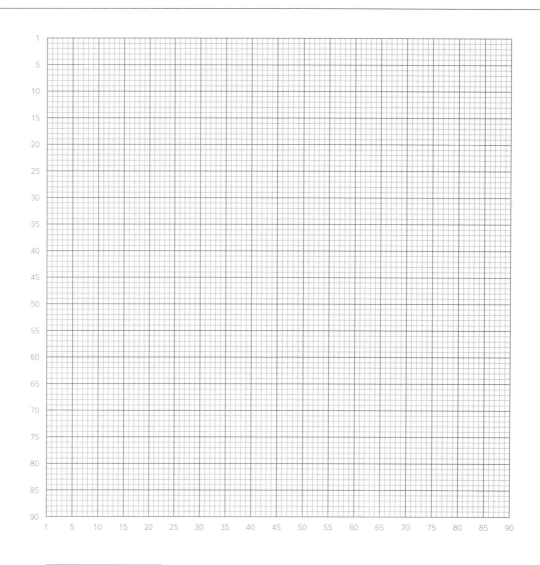

My thread colors:

☐ ☐ ☐ ☐
☐ ☐ ☐ ☐
☐ ☐ ☐ ☐
☐ ☐ ☐ ☐
☐ ☐ ☐ ☐
☐ ☐ ☐ ☐
☐ ☐ ☐ ☐

☐ I would like to embroider this.

Embroidered on: _____

Gift for: _____

I used the following materials: _____

_____

_____

_____

_____

_____

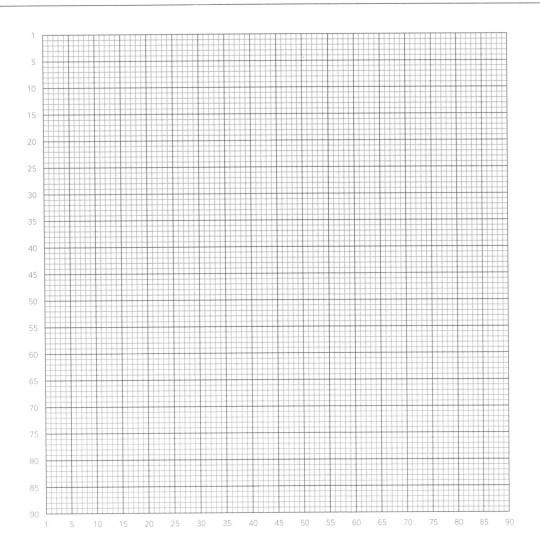

My thread colors:

☐ ☐ ☐ ☐
☐ ☐ ☐ ☐
☐ ☐ ☐ ☐
☐ ☐ ☐ ☐
☐ ☐ ☐ ☐
☐ ☐ ☐ ☐
☐ ☐ ☐ ☐

☐ I would like to embroider this.

Embroidered on: _____

Gift for: _____

I used the following materials: _____

_____

_____

_____

_____

_____

My thread colors:

☐ ☐ ☐ ☐
☐ ☐ ☐ ☐
☐ ☐ ☐ ☐
☐ ☐ ☐ ☐
☐ ☐ ☐ ☐
☐ ☐ ☐ ☐
☐ ☐ ☐ ☐

☐ I would like to embroider this.

Embroidered on: _____

Gift for: _____

I used the following materials: _____

_____

_____

_____

_____

_____

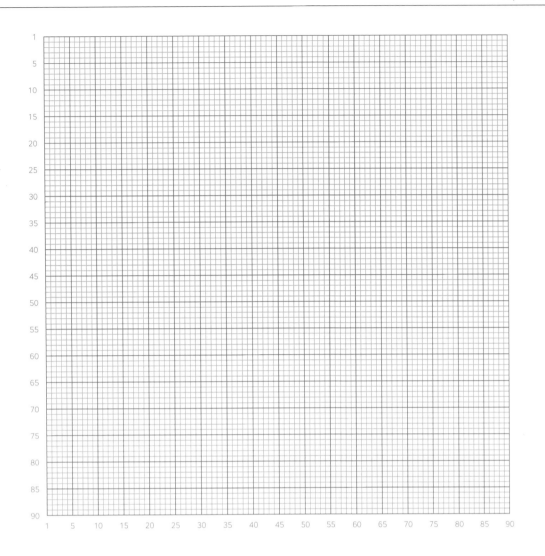

My thread colors:

☐ ☐ ☐ ☐
☐ ☐ ☐ ☐
☐ ☐ ☐ ☐
☐ ☐ ☐ ☐
☐ ☐ ☐ ☐
☐ ☐ ☐ ☐
☐ ☐ ☐ ☐

☐ I would like to embroider this.

Embroidered on: _____

Gift for: _____

I used the following materials: _____

_____

_____

_____

_____

_____

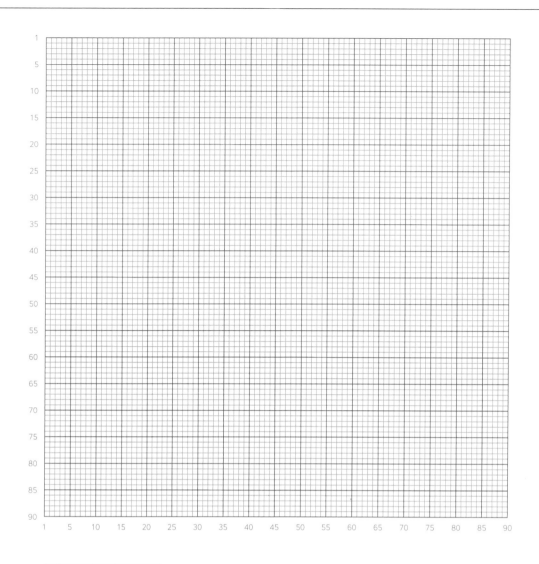

My thread colors:

☐ ☐ ☐ ☐
☐ ☐ ☐ ☐
☐ ☐ ☐ ☐
☐ ☐ ☐ ☐
☐ ☐ ☐ ☐
☐ ☐ ☐ ☐
☐ ☐ ☐ ☐

☐ I would like to embroider this.

Embroidered on: _____

Gift for: _____

I used the following materials: _____

_____

_____

_____

_____

_____

_____

✕ ✕

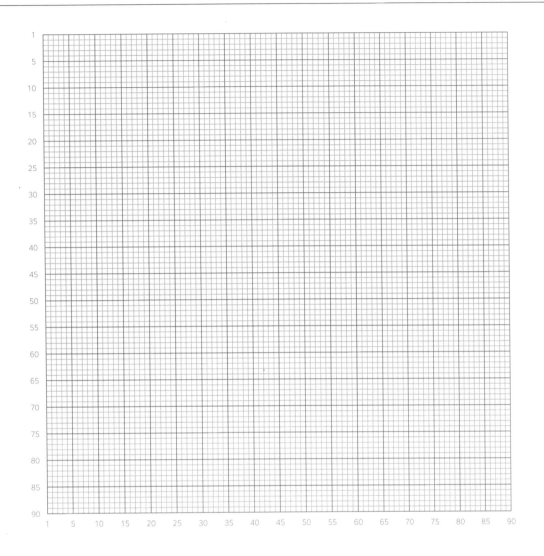

My thread colors:

☐ ☐ ☐ ☐
☐ ☐ ☐ ☐
☐ ☐ ☐ ☐
☐ ☐ ☐ ☐
☐ ☐ ☐ ☐
☐ ☐ ☐ ☐
☐ ☐ ☐ ☐

☐ I would like to embroider this.

Embroidered on: _____

Gift for: _____

I used the following materials: _____

_____

_____

_____

_____

_____

✕ ✕

COLOR TABLE

Anchor	DMC	
1	White	Snow White
9	352	Pale Pink
10	351	Light Red
11	350	Red-Pink
13	349	Pastel Red
19	321	Brick Red
20	816	Cherry
22	815	Dark Red
25	3716	Light Pink
28	956	Strawberry
29	891	Magenta
36	3326	Candy Pink
39	3832	Rouge
47	321	Signal Red
48	963	Matte Pink
49	3689	Pink
60	3688	Dark Pink
62	3805	Pastel Pink
63	3804	Ice Pink
69	3803	Dark Berry
70	3685	Berry Mix
72	902	Bordeaux
74	3354	Baby Pink
75	3733	Cotton Candy
76	3731	Bubblegum
78	917	Watermelon
79	3687	Aubergine
86	3608	Bright Pink
89	917	Wild Berry
94	917	Berry
103	153	Light Lavender
109	209	Vivid Lilac
111	208	Vivid Purple

Anchor	DMC	
112	3837	Violet
117	341	Baby Blue
118	156	Vivid Light Blue
119	333	Blue-Purple
121	794	Light Blue
122	3807	Deep Blue
129	3325	Pastel Blue
131	798	Blue
132	797	Deep Sea Blue
133	796	Midnight Blue
134	820	Navy
139	797	Ocean Blue
140	3755	Sea Blue
142	798	Marine Blue
143	797	Mid-Blue
145	799	Dark Sea Blue
148	311	Dark Blue
150	336	Blue-Black
159	162	Cloudy Blue
162	517	Deep Sea Blue
169	3760	Petrol Blue
185	959	Pastel Turquoise
186	186	Classic Turquoise
187	3851	Turquoise
188	3812	Dark Turquoise
189	3850	Mint
203	954	Light Leaf Green
204	913	Light Grass Green
205	911	Frog Green
208	563	Soft Green
210	505	Vivid Dark Green
212	561	Dark Grass Green
215	320	Woodruff

Anchor	DMC	
218	319	Moss
226	702	Leafy Forest
229	910	Fir Tree
230	909	Vivid Green
231	453	Washed-Out White
232	452	Matte Light Gray
234	762	Light Mouse-Gray
235	414	Mouse-Gray
238	703	Apple Green
243	988	Bright Fir Tree
244	987	Fir Green
246	986	Leafy Green
275	746	Ecru
290	444	Sunny Yellow
291	444	Vivid Sunny Yellow
292	3078	Light Yellow
295	3822	Lime
298	972	Deep Yellow
300	745	Pastel Yellow
301	743	Honey Yellow
302	743	Dark Honey Yellow
305	3821	Lemon Yellow
306	3820	Light Mustard
307	3852	Mustard
308	783	Dark Mustard
309	782	Warm Light Brown
310	781	Hazelnut
311	780	Warm Yellow
313	434	Warm Lime
316	3827	Tangerine
324	721	Ginger
326	720	Coral
328	3341	Salmon
330	947	Bright Orange
333	900	Pumpkin
335	606	Orange
336	3771	Powder
337	3778	Rosé
338	3778	Dark Rosé
339	920	Rust Orange
340	919	Dark Rust
341	918	Classic Rust Red

Anchor	DMC	
342	211	Lilac
347	3064	Greige
349	3826	Dark Red-Brown
355	975	Cinnamon
357	433	Espresso
358	3862	Chocolate
359	801	Dark Brown
360	898	Soft Brown
361	738	Apricot
362	437	Desert Sand
367	738	Caramel
369	435	Light Red-Brown
370	780	Classic Brown
375	869	Caramel Brown
376	3864	Light Beige
378	3861	Straw
379	3860	Deep Beige
386	3823	Light Lemon
398	415	Light Gray
399	318	Gray
400	317	Anthracite
403	310	Black
779	3786	Petrol Green
848	927	Gray-White
850	926	Light Petrol
851	924	Deep Petrol
859	523	Deep Khaki
860	522	Khaki
868	758	Pink-Beige
870	3042	Light Purple
875	3813	Lime Green
876	3816	Plant Green
877	3815	Deep Green
878	501	Dark Pastel Green
879	500	Dark Green
882	758	Sand
883	3064	Rosé-Brown
888	3045	Waffle
890	729	Eggshell
891	3825	Cognac
892	225	Teint
893	224	Powder

Anchor	DMC	
895	223	Vivid Pink
896	3721	Vivid Pink II
903	3032	Beech
914	3859	Creamy Beige
920	932	Light Gray-Blue
921	931	Gray-Blue
922	930	Dark Gray-Blue
923	3818	Cactus
933	543	Light Apricot
944	869	Light Brown
968	778	Creamy Pink
969	152	Classic Dusky Pink
970	3687	Matte Berry
977	334	Ice Blue
978	322	Sky
979	312	Dark Blue
1003	3853	Autumn Leaves
1007	3772	Warm Wood
1014	335	Rust
1016	3727	Warm Dusky Pink
1017	316	Dusky Pink
1023	3712	Pink
1024	3328	Coral Red
1027	3722	Deep Dusky Pink
1028	3685	Vivid Wild Berry
1031	3753	Snow Crystal
1039	518	Ocean
1048	3776	Golden Yellow
1066	3809	Petrol
1074	3814	Dark Turquoise
1076	3847	Emerald
1082	841	Gray Beige
1084	840	Honey-Brown
1092	964	Light Turquoise
1098	3801	Circus Red
5975	356	Rust Red
9046	321	Red
9159	3841	Sleet
9575	758	Pink-Gray

ABOUT THE AUTHOR

Jennifer Dargel is the artist behind the Sonntagskreativität (Sunday Creativity) label. She lives with her husband, son, and cat in Düsseldorf, where she also studied. She founded Sonntagskreativität after having worked in the press and events industry for several years. What initially started as a creative weekend escape has now become a real passion. Her love for embroidery hoops began in 2015 and has remained ever since. Today, she designs and stitches modern embroidery art which she successfully shares with her followers on Instagram. It's not just her individual cross-stitch family portraits that are highly popular—she's also inspired many others to get creative with her DIY embroidery boxes and hopes this book will further encourage people to do the same.

ACKNOWLEDGEMENTS

It's fair to say this book is very much a family project. When the amazing opportunity to create a cross-stitch book first came about, my son had just turned two and hadn't yet started kindergarten. That's why the first thing I want to do is thank the person who always encourages me to follow my own path in life. Who has my back even if it means taking a back seat himself. Who encourages me to seize every opportunity and supports me in word and deed. The man by my side, my partner in crime, my home—thank you for always being there!

As far as life with a child is concerned, it really does take a village. There are the grandparents who are always there to step in when I need them, no matter how much notice they are given. You're great! Thank you! There are my siblings who always have an open ear for me, especially my talented brother, who not only took all the photos for the theoretical section of the book but also ran around with me and his camera to get the perfect shots of my creations—thank you so, so much. There are my aunt and cousin who not only provide the best source of children's entertainment but who also sit in front of the TV at night whilst winding my thread or cutting out the backs of my embroidery. I couldn't have gotten this far without your help, so I'd like to say another big thank-you! Last but not least, thank you to my

embroidery "girls" who stitched their fingers to the bone while listening to a 7-hour audiobook—this book would have been nowhere near as beautiful without you.

All these people are so important and instrumental in enabling me to live out my dream here. I've had the pleasure of getting to know such wonderful, creative people in the process—first and foremost my editor, Isabella, who has always been there for me with her open, calm manner and encouraged me to believe in my talent and the quality of the end product. Thank you to her and everyone at the publishing company for making this book such a great success and for the inspiring collaboration. I would also like to thank my sponsors—Anchor, Prym, and Buttinette. Being able to pick out anything I want has always been a childhood dream of mine! And then, of course, there's my Instagram "girls," my community, some of whom have been with me for years. Let's be honest: Sonntagskreativität would not be what it is today without your support. I thank you all from the bottom of my heart.

That was long, but I like to make sure things are done properly!

Metric Conversions:

The metric measurements in this book follow standard conversion practices for sewing and soft crafts. The metric equivalents are often rounded off for ease of use. If you need more exact measurements, there are a number of amazing online converters.

365 Cross-Stitch

First published in the United States in 2023 by C&T Publishing, Inc., P.O. Box 1456, Lafayette, CA 94549

EMF © Edition Michael Fischer GmbH, 2021

www.emf-verlag.de

This translation of 365 STICKMOTIVE – DAS VORLAGENBUCH first published in Germany by Edition Michael Fischer GmbH in 2021 is published by arrangement with Silke Bruenink Agency, Munich, Germany.

PUBLISHER: Amy Barrett-Daffin

CREATIVE DIRECTOR: Gailen Runge

SENIOR EDITOR: Roxane Cerda

ASSOCIATE EDITOR: Jennifer Warren

ENGLISH-LANGUAGE COVER DESIGNER: April Mostek

ENGLISH TRANSLATION: Chantelle Fiske

PRODUCTION COORDINATOR: Zinnia Heinzmann

COVER PHOTOGRAPHY by Katja Schubert / SHOT FOTOGRAFIE

LIFESTYLE PHOTOGRAPHY by Katja Schubert / SHOT FOTOGRAFIE and instructional photography by Lars Dargel, unless otherwise noted

ILLUSTRATIONS:
Front cover & page 3: FunnyVectorForYou/Shutterstock.com
Page 18: Sasha_astra/Shutterstock.com
Tip Box: The Noun Project / Shutterstock.com and Alexander Wiefel / Shutterstock.com

Printed in China

10 9 8 7 6 5 4 3 2 1